The
Pivot Project

Pineapple
Love!

Susie
Schaefer

The
Pivot Project

STORIES TO INSPIRE
THE SHIFT IN YOUR LIFE

SUSIE SCHAEFER

The Pivot Project: Stories to Inspire the Shift in Your Life
Published by FINISH THE BOOK PUBLISHING LLC
TEMECULA, CALIFORNIA

Trauma Alert: Some chapters may contain personal recollections of domestic violence, sexual trauma, substance abuse, racism, and topics of a sensitive nature. These accounts may trigger reactions, such as flashbacks, nightmares, panic attacks or other negative responses, and readers should take precautions. In an effort to honor the personal stories of the authors, these sensitive situations have been treated with integrity, while allowing the authors' voice to be heard. Chapters with sensitive material are noted in the Table of Contents.

SCHAEFER, SUSIE, Author
THE PIVOT PROJECT
SUSIE SCHAEFER

ISBN: 978-1-7353519-0-2

BIOGRAPHY & AUTOBIOGRAPHY / Personal Memoirs
BODY, MIND & SPIRIT / Inspiration & Personal Growth

Book Design by Michelle M. White
Editing by James M. Ranson and Amy Scott

QUANTITY PURCHASES: Schools, companies, professional groups, clubs, and other organizations may qualify for special terms when ordering quantities of this title. For information, email Info@FinishTheBookPublishing.com.

Dedication

*We dedicate this book to our dear friend
Lisa Waugh, for without your story,
ours would not be complete.*

With pineapple hugs, loving thoughts, and healing prayers,
The Pivot Project Team
Aericka, Amy, Diana, Gail, Georgia, Gregg,
James, Jane, Janene, Jedediah, Joan,
Kelly, Michelle, and Susie

"You can choose to be optimistic every day, it just takes practice. Be patient and persistent. Life is not so much what you accomplish as what you overcome."

– Robin Roberts, Good Morning America Anchor
and Cancer Survivor

Table of Contents

Introduction

In the Fall of 2019, the thought of creating an anthology featuring multiple authors with the theme of PIVOT became not just an idea, but a calling. The pull to create such a book kept coming up for me, time and again, and I knew that it would eventually come to fruition…I just didn't know how, or in what form.

Enter Spring 2020 with all its changes—going from life as usual to everything we knew being upended and the rise of a global pandemic shutting down commerce, schools and creating massive shifts in our day-to-day reality. It was the beginning of a new way of life, much to our shock and surprise.

This was the revelation I was searching for…the opportunity to create a program called *Behind the Scenes*, a six-month journey that takes aspiring authors through the process of independent publishing by writing not a whole book, but just a single chapter. Through the program, we create a book and learn the publishing process, working with editors and designers while the contributing authors learn in an educational format. The end result allows the reader of *The Pivot Project* to peek into the lives of people who share their own personal stories about embracing change by facing a pivot head on – and not knowing the final outcome.

Everyone experiences change in their lives at some point, we just don't always see it coming until it's smack in front of us, causing us to make a conscious choice whether or not to go with the flow or fight the shift in our reality. Sometimes the pivots we face take our lives in an entirely new direction, setting foot on a new path, strapped with a backpack of wisdom from our past.

Months later, as we are still in an ever-changing world, not having the vision to know what life will look and feel like in the months ahead, but gradually accepting our "new normal" to our best ability. It is with deep gratitude and appreciation that we present you with our creation, a collaboration of stories to guide you through your own personal pivot story. I am humbled by the dedication of the authors as they share themselves with you.

These are their stories.

- Susie Schaefer, Founder
Finish the Book Publishing

Navigating Happiness

They had predicted fifty-knot winds. I knew I was safe with my boat around me. I had gone to bed about ten knowing the sounds of the impending storm might keep me awake for a while.

The sound of clanking halyards was deafening. I cuddled myself even further inside my down comforter to reassure myself all was right with the world. The boat was rocking wildly from side to side but I knew the five lines that had me tied to the dock were secure—I had checked them earlier in the day knowing the storm would be in all its glory about midnight.

Just rock yourself to sleep, close your eyes, all is good. The boat and I had made a pact fifteen years ago that I would take care of her and she would take care of me. She was now forty-two years old and I was much older. The goal was to keep us both looking good on the outside and functioning well on the inside. Trust is big in any relationship, even with my boat. She loved me and I loved her, full stop.

It was the first week of the COVID-19 quarantine. My sister had begged me to fly to New Jersey and spend the quarantine at our house at the Jersey shore. I thought about it for a half a second. Actually, it was a tease because there was no place I would rather be quarantined than surrounded by my boat and the things that make me feel secure and at peace. I had been sick on the boat before with the flu under self-quarantine, and I knew my own home was where I wanted to be.

Nobody knew how this virus was going to change our lives. Most folks who lived part-time on their boats returned to onshore housing, moving to homes in such places as Utah, Arizona, Hawaii, you name it. A few of us chose to stay. I was alone with my thirty-six-foot floating yacht, *Principal Interest*, along with the maintenance crew of the yacht club and my trusty green Prius that was filled with gas, ready to go to a grocery store or market if need be.

Two days before the storm I began to assess what I needed to survive for two weeks with the world's smallest refrigerator and even smaller spaces to store things. We all assumed we must have contracted the airborne surface-clinging monster somewhere in our travels around humans just before the quarantine. My protective gear was limited to my racing gloves, no masks, one bandana, no thermometer, plenty of medication, a week's worth of food, a dozen bottles of Cabernet Sauvignon, two rolls of paper towels, and access to Amazon, which kept telling me the items I needed were available but then apologized for being out of stock at this time.

I spent many days reflecting on my life during those first fourteen days. I had a half dozen forks in the road in which I knew the decisions I made had a significant impact on my life. Most turned out good, others not so good. All I knew was I was getting older and I was trying hard not to have "not good" continue impacting my life. Although my decision to buy and live on a boat was not a smart decision monetarily (boats depreciate in value and can be a money pit), it was without a doubt the wisest decision I had ever made as a free-spirited woman. There were no regrets here.

I always had a propensity to live near the water. I lived my childhood in New Jersey where there were 120 miles of barrier beach. Every year, after eighteen, I moved out of my family's home in North Jersey and would venture south to a little town named Avon by the Sea and would rent a room in a boarding-house with a view of the ocean. I spent my days waitressing to pay for my room and board and came out a few hundred dollars ahead to help get started with clothes and supplies for the fall semester of college.

I got married to my best friend after we both graduated from college, thinking this was how things were done. This Pivot Point turned out to be not such a good choice. We were too young. We hadn't even explored who we were yet and shortly after our marriage Daniel broke the news that he never wanted to have children. *I don't know why we never discussed this before marriage; I just assumed it.* I felt trapped in a room without air. I saw an ad in the *New York Times* searching for teachers to come to Australia. It said that New South Wales was experiencing a severe teacher shortage. Daniel agreed to a quick no-fault divorce and we moved on with our lives.

Getting on the plane to Sydney, Australia, was one of the biggest Pivot Points of my life. It truly was the most freeing experience for sure. Yes, I had a job, but I was now a free spirit beholden to none. I liked it. Of course, I took a look around Sydney; water was everywhere but I wanted the water close enough to walk to. I found Bondi Beach and set up a flat with a colorful American girl from Connecticut named Lacy.

I decided Australia was going to be my new forever home. However, you know what they say, "God laughs when you are making plans." I was in search of adventure and my soul mate who would love to travel and perhaps we'd sail the seven seas together.

I fell in love at first sight when I met my co-worker. He looked like Burt Reynolds and was just as cheeky. However, I found out quickly he was married and for the next few years we worked together as partners in the world of mutual respect. As life would have it, he separated from his wife of ten years and filed for divorce. We distanced ourselves for a short while but there was this mutual attraction that drew us together.

We began to live together in a small flat in Sydney and decided on sharing a bigger project renovating a century-old house in the little peninsula town of Balmain close to Sydney. Brad was a stalwart Aussie. He grew up as a country boy and had a great love for hunting in the Outback. I loved the adventure and the thrill of hunting in the scrub. We spent a lot of time with his family. However, three years of renovating and teaching in the same classroom every day took its toll on us. Brad shocked me one day with the news that he needed a break and was moving to Ontario, Canada, for a year as an exchange teacher.

"What kind of break?" I asked, rubbing back tears.

"You know, the kind where you do your thing and I do mine," he said. "You have had lots of adventures in your life and I need one too."

I expected he would find his way back to me. He was my anchor in life and I deeply loved him, but as fate would have it, a man I knew to be a player and hustler began knocking on my door. You either loved this wild Texan or you hated him. Most of the girls loved him because he looked like Mel Gibson. He was handsome and arrogant and he knew it. It was the world according to Wyatt Stetson. I knew I was attracted to his looks but not his behavior. He had dated my friend Lacy off and on for years but he treated her badly, which made me suspicious of his respect for all women. However, all this flew into the wind one night. Passion consumed me the moment Wyatt and I became intimate. Endorphins are funny things. Whether you are hooked on drugs or desire, the trap is always the same; you can't crave it enough and you live for the next fix.

My life was twisted into need and passion. I tried to end the relationship, knowing it could never last, when he shocked me by asking me to be the mother of his children. Fate had taken a turn and following my heart was leading me down a dark rabbit hole. Wyatt moved in with me.

One morning before heading off to work there was a knock. I opened the front door wide and my heart hit my knees. It was Brad. After several months with Wyatt I had written Brad a letter to explain the current circumstances, with the intent of not wanting him to hear the news from someone else. Brad wasn't due back until December; it was only August.

"Oh my God, what are you doing here?" I asked, shaking. I told him Wyatt was upstairs and asked if he could come back in an hour. I quickly called the school for a substitute. I kept pacing the floor wondering why he'd come back. I knew he was on his summer break—he had written that he was doing a car trip across Canada with a girl. Did he have the girl with him? I found myself feeling slightly jealous. I clearly still loved Brad, but passion had consumed me into a love that clouded all judgment. It was based on need.

Brad returned and we began a casual friendly conversation about his year in Ontario and his trip through Canada. Finally, I asked, "So is your girlfriend here? You didn't leave her sitting out there in the car, did you?"

"No, and she isn't my girlfriend," he said. "She's just a girl I work with who wanted to tour Canada with someone. She headed back to Toronto when I said I was going to fly back to Sydney for a while."

I was still confused about why he was there until he edged closer to me and got down on one knee. My mind was screaming, *NO! You're not going to do this now. Please don't let this be the moment I waited for all these years.*

His words came out slowly. "So, I never asked you this one question... Will you marry me?" My mouth froze open like the Edvard Munch picture *The Scream.* I couldn't say anything. I could only shake. "Tell me it's not too late, please, it can't be too late."

I was shaking uncontrollably and all I could utter was, "I think it is." *It was the perfect proposal at exactly the wrong time.*

Brad got understandably angry. "I just flew 10,000 miles across the Pacific to propose to you. You need to think long and hard about this," he yelled, slamming the front door shut as he left the house. My life was climaxing into my biggest Pivot Point of all.

Brad returned to Sydney in December, two months after Wyatt had left for the States. Wyatt had lost his restaurant in a court battle and decided Sydney was dead for him. He told me he was heading for the prettiest place on earth: Ruidoso, New Mexico.

I applied for a leave of absence for a year from the government of New South Wales starting in June. I planned to join Wyatt in New Mexico as soon as he left me a way to contact him. I thought for sure Brad would have given up on me. *How does one recover after being rejected from a marriage proposal?* He visited me often and somehow, we ended up living together for the next six months in the house we had renovated. I thought for sure having Brad back would allow me to be free of the passion I felt for Wyatt. The passion was distant, but never gone.

I was clearly in love with two men at the same time, but differently. One was my anchor and trusted companion and the other filled me with passion and excitement. I couldn't choose. *I knew what the smart choice should be.* However, I had convinced myself that even shady men wanted good women beside them to help raise their children. I already had a plane ticket to the States. I told Brad I needed to go and figure this out. I just knew Wyatt would be playing around and unsettled and it would be easy for me to come back and put him behind me. I also knew I would be unsettled in my relationship with Brad if I didn't get past my passion for Wyatt. *Was I opening Pandora's box?*

I recognized early in my life that one of the strongest parts of my personality was that I was a risk taker. I did look for the quicksand before I would leap but didn't always see it in advance. I walked onto the plane in late June never looking back. Immediately my life's compass shifted north when I had always visualized it south. Within weeks of my arrival in New Mexico Wyatt and I were married and a month later I was pregnant with the first of our two sons.

The marriage didn't last. Wyatt was quickly absent and the real Pivot Point became clear: life as a single mom of two boys. The Pivot Point to follow Wyatt hadn't been the best one. It led me down a road to a hard life alone raising two sons without much support. *Seeking your soul mate can be tricky business.* News from friends a few years later said that Brad had settled down with an Aussie gal and they had two daughters. My destiny now sat in the Northern Hemisphere. I moved out of the mountains of New Mexico to raise the boys in Southern California because again, it was close to the water. We settled in a beach community in the San Diego area.

I took greater stock in my educational career. I recognized now that my number-one job was to raise two good men. I worked hard at it. My experiences as a single mom helped me create relationships with mothers as I became a principal. I surrounded myself with passionate people who worked diligently at their craft. Our dedication paid off as we took a gang school with low scores to become a California Distinguished School.

In what seemed like no time at all my boys grew old enough to leave home. I now owned a condo and my life was in order, but I was still very unsettled. I had always dreamed of going off to sea and traveling around the world on water. However, the reality was I was much older now and all these years of being single hadn't resulted in me finding my soul mate. I knew I was a romantic and although life was not over yet, the reality was this lingering image of life on the water continually fed my soul. I decided that instead of trying to build a life near the water, which was millions of dollars out of my reach, I could afford to be *on* the water by purchasing a boat and living aboard. I began to look around at boats. It was a ten-year plan. By some twist of fate, I found my three-level motor yacht, a two-bedroom, two-bath condo which was to be my new tiny house on the water.

In the year of my youngest son's eighteenth birthday I made the announcement to my two sons. "I know both of you are off to live your dreams and build your future, but so am I. I'm selling the condo and buying a thirty-six-foot motor yacht. I know sometimes children come back to live with their parents. I just want you both to know you are *always* welcome to come home but your room will now be limited to a 'V' berth in the front of my boat." Although they visited from time to time, neither of them chose to come back to live with mom. I think in some small way this made the reality of growing up accelerate. They turned the page from boys to men rather quickly.

I was still working every day as a school administrator and I needed to rent a room from a girlfriend several days a week in order to cut down on the three-hour commute. However, my spirits would begin to lift the moment I turned the car toward the boat, and as soon as I set my foot on the docks my lungs would catch the crisp cool air off the water and a gentle "ahh" would escape my lips.

At first, I was in a marina where they did not allow people to live aboard. I came down every weekend and every Wednesday night so that I could also race sailboats in the local Beer Can Races. I quickly became a passionate late-blooming sailor. I know my decision to live on the water was the biggest Pivot Point of all. I traded the security of money for a future dream of living on the water. The wind, the sea, and my boat brought me the much-needed balance I yearned for in my everyday life and the peace I was looking for that only nature can provide.

<hr/>

Thirty-six years after I had boarded the plane to the States leaving Brad standing in Sydney airport I was invited to a reunion in Ontario, Canada. Five of the teachers who taught in Sydney in 1981 were getting together because two of them had booked passage on a Lancaster Bomber from WWII for a joyride. When I heard Brad was going to be one of the participants, I quickly made plans to join the group for the reunion. I spent two days reminiscing with the girls, but as soon as Brad arrived people gave us space. For the next few days, we explored the explosion I left in our lives. There were wounds that were in need of closure. We walked five miles every morning, and we stayed up into the wee hours around the kitchen table catching up on our lives after the others went to bed.

This was a moment that many people don't get to experience in life; it was a gift. I remember reading a note left anonymously in a village in Croatia that said, "Don't spend too much time thinking over your past mistakes just because you spent so much time creating them." So true, I thought, but in reality, Brad and I were still perplexed by how destiny guided us one way when clearly we still loved each other. How and why did it happen?

In my youth I was a basketball player. In basketball you rely on a pronounced pivot to change your direction to pass cleanly to other players. Wyatt was a pivot like the Pac-Man character in the game who hit me from the side and turned my compass in a completely different direction. We both wondered if this unsuspected episode was our destiny. Brad was destined to marry an Australian girl. We were both destined to have two children, he two girls, and me two boys. But I somehow got to live a life alone and not see the world through his eyes. It saddened me. We confessed to each other there wasn't a day we didn't think of each other, but my choice to pursue passion left us in different worlds. We parted friends.

Three years after the reunion, while lying in my comfy little aft cabin on the boat in the middle of the COVID-19 virus, I was looking through the Internet and a passage came across the screen like many of them often do. It said, "A friend once told me that the biggest danger to an adventurous spirit is stability and security. A free spirit needs to look for a new horizon every morning." I read the phrase over and over. It was an aha moment for me.

I knew early in life that I was adventurous and free-spirited, but when faced with one of the biggest decisions of one's life I couldn't choose my anchor because it meant stability and security. I feared it was the death of my free spirit.

They say our fears guide our lives, and so I jumped on the plane and married the one man who wouldn't provide me *any* stability or security. I suddenly realized it was all my fault. When we were living together, I once asked Brad if he thought we might get married. He laughed and said, "You're a Yank; if I married you, one day you might just get up and leave me and go home." I thought his words were stated over *his* fears but in reality, he probably sensed my nature.

A few days later I was watching a movie and another golden line leaped out to me that said, "We can't run from who we are, our destiny finds us." I know I was meant to have my two sons and knew the job I was destined to do. I also knew I was supposed to play a part in affecting so many other lives, but destiny for me was to be in the Northern Hemisphere, not the Southern Hemisphere where I had visualized my life.

COVID-19 gave me time to pause and ponder my pivotal choices. It caused me to wonder whether they were really my choices or whether our compasses are already set from the start. Without a doubt my life on a boat defined me. It certainly isn't a secure life. It continues to be a liability, depreciates yearly, and is a money pit for repairs. It will continue to be a harder life when you think about it.

For fifteen years I have owned this beautiful maiden. She is now the anchor in my life. She comes with no security or stability. Getting on board is always an adventure with an unsure future. I appreciate each and every day because we both know our days are numbered. I'll sink more money into strengthening her survival in the hopes it will strengthen mine. I pray we both get many more years rocking in the bay, watching the birds, witnessing the sunrise and the sunset, being the master and commander of our world.

❖

A native of New Jersey who flew off to travel the world and find herself in 1975, Georgia Faye found an ad in the *New York Times* to fill a severe teacher shortage in New South Wales, Australia. This decision was one of the biggest pivot points of her life.

While in Australia, Georgia fell in love three times: first with Australia itself (vowing never to leave), then with a stalwart Aussie teacher who shared his intimacy and his love of the Outback, and finally a wild Texan player and hustler who filled her life with passion and excitement. As a young woman she would tell others, "I'm low maintenance, easy to live with but I'm complicated."

Georgia has lived in the San Diego area for thirty years, fifteen of those on her forty-year-old motor yacht. Her twenty-five-year career in education led her to be recognized for an abundance of major awards for community development, including acknowledgments from the Chamber of Commerce, Zero Waste, STEM schools, farm to table, and two Distinguished School Awards, which ultimately honored her with the title of Southern California's Principal of the Year.

Georgia is the proud mother of two beautiful sons and now has six beautiful grandchildren. She continues to pursue an adventurous life traveling the world and volunteering for international volunteer programs in Europe and West Kenya.

Georgia has been writing creatively for years and is in the process of publishing her breakout novel *Down Under*. She is a member of the San Diego Writers/Editors Guild, Writer's Digest, the Authors Guild, and Romance Writers of America. You can contact Georgia Faye at phyllis.captmorgan@gmail.com.

Jane Hinshaw

The Parental Pirouette

Y ou may read the title of this chapter and say to yourself, "I'm not a parent. This story isn't going to be for me." But we all have parents! And our friends have parents or are parents themselves. I believe that when we walk in someone else's shoes we not only gain a better understanding of who they have come to be, but we also understand ourselves and those we love just a little bit more. Perhaps my story will help you understand what your parents went through, or maybe it will help you navigate your own parental path in the future.

I began taking ballet lessons at the age of six. I loved the fluidity of movement, the gracefulness, and the precision of the dance. The costumes only enhanced the experience and gave us renewed excitement after repeating the choreographed dances again and again in rehearsal. My teachers were always exceptional and gave me not only dance lessons, but also life lessons:

- Practice makes perfect and you're usually not perfect, so keep practicing.
- Don't peek through the curtain because it's not professional.
- Show up on time, in the right costume, and with your hair in a wispy-free bun.
- Not everyone gets the starring roles.
- Creating together is an amazing experience.

In my teen years, I was fortunate to have a family who sacrificed much and a dance teacher who took groups of kids to Japan to perform and stay in host family homes in our international sister city. The effect of these trips on my life was profound. Needless to say, my life and dance were a very tightly woven and strong foundation for whom I was to become in my adult life. Yes, I was one of the kids that said, "Dance is MY LIFE," and I really meant it.

My dream in high school, not surprisingly, was to become a professional dancer. I took ballet classes most days of the week and homework was done late at night. I enrolled in dance classes outside my home studio to broaden my somewhat narrow dance repertoire and experience teachers with different methods of instruction. But fate was not playing.

The Rockettes derailed my dream. Or at least my poor imitation of them did, resulting in a pretty severe ankle sprain. Having landed one of the major roles in the musical *Babes in Arms* at my high school (yes, a singing and *dancing* lead), I was so excited about the role I never once let on that an understudy may need to take over my part. Every performance began hours earlier for me with the taping of the injured ankle. After the performance, the tape would be cut off and the ankle would swell. It is amazing that I was able to perform. While I managed this injury, I realized I had no other plans for the future should another injury come along. I also began to seriously evaluate what a dancer's life was like and admit the length of my career would be very short. The chances of landing those lead roles was extremely slim, and speaking of slim, did I really want to starve myself to have the body type that was expected? Maybe going to college, as my parents were strongly suggesting, was the better option for me?

Allow me to explain the dance terms "pirouettes" and "pivots." A pirouette is a spin on one foot, and generally a complete rotation of your body. Typically, the other foot is raised to the knee of the spinning leg to stabilize your center of gravity. Sometimes, to add complexity, the non-spinning leg is outstretched or used as a whip to propel revolution after revolution. A pivot can be described as leaving one or both feet in place and rotating your body, usually to face your body in the opposite direction. Dance teachers would tell us to nail one foot to the floor and turn as if that nail was the pivot point. Similar to a pirouette, a pivot leaves you in the same place on the floor but allows your body to rotate—it doesn't travel. A pirouette stays in one place with your body winding up back where it started. A pivot can do the same, but usually leaves you facing a totally new direction, as in an "about face."

This ankle injury made me open my mind to really evaluate the direction I was headed and led me to pivot from that path to another. I went off to college and was on my own, meeting new friends, exploring new places. Dancing became less important in my life as other things seeped into my available time. I missed being on stage, so I started doing improvisation comedy at an open mic night not far from my college. My dance training helped me improvise some very interesting and physical performances!

As the story goes for many, I graduated and went off to work full-time. I fell in love and was married. The births of my two boys followed a move to Southern California and my life slowly but completely became all about them. I worked full-time and danced with my boys when they were still small enough to be held in my arms. Once the squirmy pre-kindergarten years advanced, even these short dances became a thing of the past. The transition from "pick me up, pick me up" to "put me down, put me down" is fairly rapid. As the boys grew, we chose to make a family pivot and move back to Northern California to raise them.

My career path continued in local government, usually in positions that had a lot of writing and budget work because I didn't mind either one. Often, I found myself making public presentations to elected bodies or to the public at informational presentations. I wanted to explore a career in law enforcement and learned that the local police academy offered a night/weekend option so I would be able to keep working at my full-time job.

I managed, with the help of my husband and children, to attend the local police academy and pivot my career. This was not easy. The physical portions of the academy are much harder when you are in your late thirties! The learning portion was the easiest part for me, but I was working full-time, trying to still be an involved mom, and going to the police academy at night and on weekends. Studying and practicing were often done with my kids so I could accomplish two things at once.

Our lives shifted as my work schedule changed. Graveyard weekday shifts meant I got to take my kids to school and pick them up, but graveyard weekend shifts meant trying to keep the kids occupied, yet quiet, so I could sleep. Just as we would get used to the schedule, it would change, and we'd have to adjust again. Thankfully I earned the promotion to detective after only eleven months on the job and was soon working a mostly permanent weekday shift.

I spent much of my time fully immersed in everything that was my family. I was *that mom* who managed to work full-time and still volunteer for every supporting role in their kids' endeavors. Need a team mom? Pick me! Snack bar operations? I'm your gal! Booster parent? I'm all in! Fundraising? Yes! Chaperone? Of course (even if my child wasn't excited about having me come along)! Want me to bring a patrol car to school and talk about my job? Just tell me what day works for you! I wanted them to soak up as much as they could, to have diverse experiences like I'd had in my childhood, and to see a big world. I was determined to help make those things happen with my own time and energy.

Dance had long been placed beyond the back burner; in fact, there was only time for me dancing with the vacuum cleaner and occasionally on the job to establish rapport with kids or get a driver's attention when directing traffic. I kept offering to teach my boys how to dance, but I was rapidly approaching the years when they looked at me as if I was joking and the offer shouldn't be taken seriously. I accepted that this was all part of the growing up process, the slow and methodical cutting of the apron strings, my little ones moving on into the lives they would shape for themselves.

My boys grew up. As much as I tried to hang on to them at every stage, they just kept growing and I loved seeing them achieving new things. Before they could drive, I cherished those moments when they were trapped in the car with me. On occasion when I was reading in bed, one would stop in and we would have an amazing chat. I was once again connected to them in the ways that I knew would become fewer. I wanted them to live their own lives and forge their own futures, but I so loved being an integral part of their lives every day. I knew letting go would be one of the hardest things I'd ever do.

My husband had given me the gift of airplane flight lessons. I spent many hours studying weather, aeronautics, FAA flight rules, airspace rules, and emergency procedures. I learned how to calculate the center of gravity for my aircraft as well as how much fuel and passenger load I could carry. I practiced maneuvers with my flight instructor and I eventually earned my pilot's certificate. I loved the change of perspective I got from being up in the air at 5,000 feet looking down at the world below. If I was having a bad day, a flight always put me into a more relaxed and grateful attitude. I loved to say, "The altitude affects my attitude."

Flying mirrored many aspects of dancing for me. You had to practice to keep up your skills. There is a sense of gracefulness as you maneuver the plane left, right, up, or down. You could have a special shared moment with others. It can be challenging, mentally and physically. You get better with someone watching and critiquing your efforts. But flying was also much more work and time than many other hobbies. You can dance anywhere, anytime and even without the benefit of music. To fly, the weather has to cooperate, the plane has to be in good working condition, the fuel has to be available and financially feasible, you have to be prepared for an emergency landing, and you have maintenance to perform on the airplane before and after the flight. A one-hour flight meant adding an hour or two before and after the flight.

Still trying to be a cool and involved mom, I took my oldest son and his girlfriend on a short ride. In the field across from her house, my youngest son and my husband had placed a huge sign. The sign read, "PROM?" and I circled over the area so she could read the sign and see her mom standing on the front porch waving at us. For a few weeks I enjoyed the cool mom status, but it faded over time, as did his need for my help or input. While you know your children will grow up and detach, it is still a painful process for the parent.

So, as wonderful as flying was, the time and the cost were issues. College for my children was also expensive, and I couldn't justify financially committing to both. I hung up my wings but kept the logbook and the memories forever.

As predicted, the oldest son left for college and I immediately felt his absence. Leaving him in his new dorm room and driving hundreds of miles back home was so much harder than I had anticipated. And yet, I was also so excited to see him embarking on this journey, full of new experiences and people. The concern about his well-being and adjustment to his new life were certainly swirling through my mind, but more than that I knew that his life was more completely separate from mine than ever before. These mixed emotions were very strong and confusing, moving from joy and excitement to worry and loss in split seconds.

I tried not to overcompensate by smothering the youngest son, but this was challenging for me! I was a police officer and used to taking charge of a situation and controlling the environment for everyone's safety. Yet this was beyond my control and none of my training and experience had prepared me for this transition. I thought about my own mother and found a new respect for what she had gone through with her three daughters. I have a much greater appreciation for my mom with these experiences because I understand at a deeper level the hard parts she's lived through raising her children. Walking in her shoes, I can understand her experience better.

I realized I needed to bring old and new hobbies and interests back into my life. I decided that one of the things I was having difficulty doing was going someplace on my own. For almost *twenty years* I was always with at least one other member of my family, if not all of them. I decided to take a trip, on my own, and challenge myself.

I started on that trip at least four times.

I got a little further each time, but it wasn't until after the failed third attempt that I really began to scold myself. "You are a grown woman who has accomplished much in her life and has never let anything intimidate her. What is the problem with getting yourself to this destination? You just point the car in the right direction and go. Stop putting up the barriers. Turn away from the fear! And while we are at it, what exactly are you afraid of happening? Nothing can happen that you can't handle!" This pep-talk actually helped get me all the way to my destination.

Then the biggest pivotal moment of my life smacked me in the head. I was standing in front of the signboard listing the sandwich options in a deli. The voice in my head was evaluating the sandwich choices: "If I pick that one and my youngest son doesn't like the one he chooses, we could switch..."

WHAM!

The realization felt like a shockwave from my head to my toes. I was alone and yet making sandwich choices based on what my son likes! I was completely unable to make a sandwich choice on my own. What did I like? I could hardly recall what my own sandwich choices had been so many years ago! When did I get so out of touch with *me* and what I liked? How had my thinking become so "mom-omatic" that I failed to be able to register my own choices?

I'll admit that this moment was so profound for me that I actually began to cry. It freaked out the deli person a little, but my assurances that "it's *not* you, it's me" seemed to suffice. I began to see that I was often hiding behind my "gotta-do" list of things for my family because I wasn't prepared to go it alone. I didn't have a "me" that I was still connected to and this was also one of the reasons the empty nest was a potential bottomless pit for me.

These self-realizations were pretty big. This was the moment I recognized I had to make the pivot. I had to re-establish who I was—not just "mom" or "wife" or "family member." I needed to recall what I liked to do, what I liked to eat, or where I liked to go visit. But an even bigger realization was that my failure to do so would mean that I would drag my kids down. They would feel bad about leaving, they would feel bound to visit, they would feel the weight of my happiness being dependent on them. No child should feel responsible for their parents' happiness and well-being. It is our responsibility to take care of ourselves and figure out how we live a healthy and well-balanced life. Remember what they tell you on the airplane...you have to put on your own oxygen mask before you can help others!

I needed to turn, but not to travel far from my pivot point—my family. I needed to rotate so I could continue to move, to grow. This movement would keep me connected, but not confined. Just as in dance, a pivot can reverse your course or spin you to a new direction. I didn't need a reversal as much as I just needed a new angle.

It certainly wasn't that I didn't have a voice in what we did as a family. And it wasn't as if I hadn't already been thinking that this empty nest thing was going to have to be addressed. It was the depth of my current thought process and the power of giving up the essential "me" that hit me so hard. I really had no idea how fully absorbed I was in my children's lives. Yes, I probably was one of those helicopter parents, but my hovering was closer to 4,000 feet rather than 400 feet. To my children, I apologize. You really don't know what you don't know!

My pivotal moment showed me how I evolved ever so slowly with my family to making allowances for their needs, often sacrificing mine unknowingly. In fact, I had willingly given up my needs in adjustment to theirs through love! The more I did for and with them, the more I felt I was connected and showing my love and dedication to them. This can be an unhealthy and unbalanced way to live life. When a person loses themselves completely, they are placing a heavy burden on others to bring more to the relationship than is equitable.

So, what to do? I tackled my parental pivot by bringing dance back into my life. I pushed myself to use one of my first loves to grow and make the pivot happen. I sought out Latin dancing (salsa, bachata, cumbia, merengue, cha cha cha) to bring new flavors into my dance life. In turn, this taught me some new and very important lessons. These dances, when in a social setting, are typically a "lead-follow" dance where one partner leads the other through different dance moves. The "follow" role was incredibly challenging for me because I am a leader by nature and profession. My career trained me how to be a strong leader, and taking charge was expected. The need to control is in my genetic makeup, and slowly I learned how to give that up and follow. To this day, one of the greatest compliments I get as a dancer is, "You follow very well," because the struggle has been real!

Many times, I failed to fully leave the security of my old patterns and drove but halfway to a dance place before turning back. Eventually I became more confident and I began attending dance festivals where I'd take classes by day and social dance by night for an entire weekend. I struggled most with the feeling that I was selfish and not being the giving, loving person I needed to be for others. Through more introspection and honesty with myself, I understood those feelings are mere justifications for putting relationship burdens on others when you sacrifice yourself so completely that there is no "you" left any longer.

I am so grateful that dance has been there for the important times in my life. I think I can still say, "Dance is MY LIFE" as strongly as I did as a teen, but it isn't my entire focus as it was back then. And I'm certainly not entertaining a professional dance career any longer! Dance is now an integral part of my physical and mental well-being. Dance feeds my body, mind, and soul and it brings such interesting and beautiful people, experiences, and music into my life. I recognize that dance is a very important part of who I am at the core and is the best way I have found to express myself and my moods. Dance supports all aspects of my life and feeds that little performer in me. I even joined a dance team to once again experience the excitement and fun that performing gives me. I'm probably the oldest person on the team, but I'm there to show people you're never too old to do what makes you happy.

When I look back, I see that I had a pivotal moment choosing my sandwich in the deli. I had to make a directional change. But then I needed to keep energizing this direction by performing pirouettes. I needed to invest in and love myself just as much as I do others. When I'm in a healthy place, loving myself is equal or even greater than my love for another and I have kept that person free from the burden of loving me more to make up for the lack of love for myself. Our expectations of others are balanced and we are disappointed less often. For those of us taught to be selfless and of service to others, we struggle with this concept. Loving yourself is not selfish, because we have an infinite supply of love!

The parental pirouette is one of those things in life that we have to do as a parent. First, we pivot away from ourselves and towards the new life we have welcomed. Slowly our pirouettes gain momentum and our children become our everything because we love them so very much. Then, as they grow up and move into their own lives, we must pivot once again. These turns can be shockwave pivots that jolt and are uncomfortable. Or they can be gentle and centered pirouettes because you maintain the healthy balance between that which is you and that which you give to others.

We all have these pivotal moments in our lives. We all have times when our lightbulbs fire up and we get clarity on our experience. We all have times when we evaluate relationships and determine if they are healthy or unhealthy. Balance in life is critical, whether that is balance in what you eat, balance in what you do with your time, or balance in your relationships. And we all have choices in how we execute those pivots when we need to rebalance.

In my parental pirouette, I was initially like a frenzied dog chasing its tail, zooming around trying to capture the tip. Then I was like a plane, slowly but intentionally turning around a point. By the time my second son made the leap to college, I was pivoting and pirouetting like a professional dancer, executing the turn as if it had been practiced time and time again, my leg outstretched to add a little challenge. I guess it is true that practice makes perfect!

Think about your own pivots. How do you view them? Even if you think of them in negative terms, didn't you learn something, and did it not serve some purpose for you? Time often changes our view of a pivot we viewed as negative, but it's like the Rolling Stones song, "You Can't Always Get What You Want"... you get what you need.

We have a choice when a pivot presents itself. We can struggle, we can fight, we can fear, we can regret. Or...

We can allow the pivot to happen, we can embrace the pivot, we can seek the pivot. We can make a pivot become multiple pirouettes and gain momentum while staying tied to our center of gravity. But that pivot from one direction to another, or that rotation that brings us back to our starting point, is so important in moving our lives forward and growing as a person.

Practice your pivots in life like a dancer and they will soon become easier, more graceful, even more choreographed. Use your pivots to grow, to add new chapters to your story, to become the beautiful dancer in your life. Be able to choose a deli sandwich for yourself no matter how much you love someone else!

A retired police officer and investigator, Jane Hinshaw has long practiced her writing skills in a less creative environment. Report writing—the documentation of what work a law enforcement officer has done on an incident—is the absolute foundation of the job. The quality of the written report is how cold  cases can be reactivated, a witness's memory can be rejuvenated, and diverse professions can piece together a crime puzzle. Jane has been working at expanding her report writing skills into literary writings that go beyond "just the facts, ma'am" and engages more of the storytelling aspects of writing.

Jane worked for nearly thirty years in local government, but not only in a law enforcement capacity. She wrote competitive million-dollar grant applications, created marketing and awareness materials for new public programs, and authored various reports for elected officials. She is an accomplished public speaker and passionate about improving local communities. Her development of an ordinance that requires background checks for people working in older adults' homes won accolades and nationwide attention.

Jane is also an accomplished dancer of various styles, volunteers for the San Diego Humane Society, and serves as a part-time instructor at police academies throughout California. When not spending time watching sunsets at the beach or visiting the San Diego Zoo and Safari Park, she is finalizing construction on her "tiny home." After years of fanatically researching this global downsizing trend, Jane looks forward to living simply and writing creatively for pleasure and purpose.

I Wear Many Hats

Music fills life and all of my life has been overflowing with music. As I grew up all I could think about was being a musician and filling my world with the sound of music. Shakespeare wrote, "If *music* be the food of love, play on." Indeed, music was the food of life for me and I did play on.

It all began when I was five years old and my mother started teaching me to play the piano. She taught me how to read music and as I grew up I began taking lessons with more experienced instructors. By the time I was nine years old I started playing the flute. I took private lessons and auditioned for many competitions playing in numerous honor bands. By the time I was fourteen I was playing in the San Luis Obispo County Symphony in central California. There isn't anything more exhilarating than playing in unison with a full-piece orchestra. It is a real adrenaline rush!

Each week I would travel thirty minutes to practice with the symphony. As I was only fourteen, I would ride along with adults who played in the orchestra. One of the musicians flew a small plane and one week asked me if I wanted to fly to the orchestra rehearsal in his plane. I jumped at the chance and when we were in the plane he said, "You want to try flying the plane?" The next thing I knew he let me pilot the plane for a short time while we were in flight. This was such a thrill that I still remember it all these years later. The orchestra would put on concerts all year long and I performed with them until I was nineteen years old.

The Music Academy of the West in Montecito is considered the Juilliard of the California Coast. They have a classical music training program each summer for students and I asked my parents if I could attend. It was very expensive and at first my parents said no. I spent so much time begging them to let me go; I swore I would never ask them for anything else in my life and that I would do cleaning and the dishes every day of the year. Finally, my parents relented and I was all set to go during the summer of my seventeenth year. I slept in a house in Santa Barbara filled with many other girls. Each day we were bused to the academy where we had a day jam-packed with music. I was probably one of the least-trained musicians there so it was very inspiring to be surrounded by all of those talented artists.

The stunning gardens were a perfect place to practice each day. The estate had amazing landscaping with a beautiful koi pond. I remember that I would stroll through the pristine gardens surrounded by perfectly manicured hedges and look for a private place to practice. I was given a private lesson each week from Roger Stevens who was a flautist from the LA Philharmonic.

During the summer I practiced five hours a day. I noticed that the pianists practiced ten hours a day to acquire the skills they needed to be a professional musician. They would bring their lunch with them and just practice and practice and practice! I thought to myself, *thank goodness I didn't decide to be a professional pianist because I can be a professional flautist and only practice half the time!* The academy overlooked the ocean and at the end of the day I would find my way down to the beach and hang out with some of the other musicians.

After graduating from high school, I decided to attend the local junior college in San Luis Obispo and work on receiving an Associate of Arts degree in music. I lived in a dorm and continued my pursuits in music. The next summer I was living in the dorm when most of the other students were gone. One day I was practicing my flute and apparently the music traveled over quite a distance. All of a sudden as I was playing, two girls came over to see where the music was coming from. It was two students who were never friendly towards me. When they came around the corner and saw me they were shocked. They complimented me on my playing and we were friends from that moment on! At that point, I realized the healing powers music has on people.

I graduated with a music degree and went on to a four-year college at Cal Poly San Luis Obispo, where I met my husband. We married and had a child, but it was not meant to be. My husband passed away when I was only twenty-four. I graduated from Cal Poly and as a single mother I chose to travel with my girlfriend Becky Silver. She also had a child and we were out for an adventure and to see if we could discover what we wanted to do with the rest of our lives. I traveled to Mexico and Central America with Becky. I had the pleasure of meeting Christiane Nazzi who was playing with the Guadalajara Philharmonic. I was thrilled to meet her. She was from the United States and I was excited to chat with her about a career in music. She said it was very hard to be hired as a woman because you were looked upon at that time as if you would get married, get pregnant, and quit. For that reason, they didn't want to hire women and that is why she had to seek a job outside of the United States. It seemed like it was getting harder and harder to have a career in music.

When I returned to the U.S. I relocated to San Diego. At that time, there were already two flutes in the San Diego Symphony Orchestra, so I had to rethink another way of earning a living. I formed duos with classical guitarists and a harpist. We would play at weddings, parties, receptions, renaissance fairs, and restaurants. I began teaching piano and flute at a music store on Balboa Avenue in San Diego and loved teaching both adults and children. During this period, I studied jazz and composition with Bud Conway, a San Diego legend. I worked with him for ten years and even wrote a ballet.

As time progressed, I branched out and the harpist Vicki McMasters and I put together an all-girl rock-and-roll band. McMasters played piano and I played flute and tenor saxophone. We added a guitar player, a bass guitar, and of course a singer. It was so much fun playing in the band, practicing each week in a garage and then going out to perform in clubs. At one point an agent came down from Los Angeles and wanted to book us to play in the Holiday Inn hotels around the country. The agent previously had a group named Heather that had disbanded, so we would be under contract with that name and travel around playing in the hotels. Since I was a single mother, I couldn't see myself travelling around trying to find babysitters in other cities throughout the country, so I gave an emphatic no to the group. Some of the members of the band wanted to accept his offer so our group fizzled out.

Two other exciting events in my musical career were performing each night (costume and all) in the play *Poor Murderer* at the Cassius Carter Centre Stage in Balboa Park. I wrote a piece of music that was recorded and played every night as the actors arrived on stage. Sometimes during our break, I would hear the other actors whistling or humming the tune that I had written. It was so gratifying to know how much they enjoyed it. I also performed in the play *Twelfth Night* at the Patio Playhouse in Escondido.

It was about this time when my music career flatlined. It felt like I was standing outside on a beautiful day with a clear bright sky and all of a sudden an ominous dark cloud came over, casting a huge shadow on my life. *What happened? How could this be?*

In the music industry, DJs started spinning vinyl records. They began booking a majority of our business playing at parties and weddings and taking most of the gigs we used to get. They were considered talented celebrities who people couldn't wait to hire. This was considered a super-star industry with die-hard fans. All I could think about was what was their skill level, experience, and how many hours did they practice a day on the turntables? I had practiced five hours a day since I was a child and I was being replaced? How could it get any worse? The musicians I performed with didn't want to play with me anymore because there were so few jobs; they wanted to play solo so they could keep all the profits. Harpists and guitarists can play both melody and harmony, so they didn't need me anymore. I could only play melody so I needed them. There were very few occasions where someone would request that I play flute only at their wedding. Indeed, the next chapter of my life had begun.

I pondered what other skills I had and recalled how much I loved sewing from an early age when I was in the 4-H club. I began sewing for other people and then decided to try to get a job in the Costume Department at the Old Globe theater. I loved working there with all the actors and having the opportunity to watch their brilliant productions. I have always had a fondness for headwear, but the hats in the department stores were always too small for my head. I thought I would love to learn how to make them, so I asked the Costume Department if I could go into the Millinery Department where they made hats. To my delight there was an opening as Assistant Milliner. I learned how to make almost every shape and style of hat from felt to straw and even fur. It gave me the opportunity to work with famous actors such as Marsha Mason, Patti LuPone, Victor Garber, David Ogden Stiers, Larry Drake, and Harry Groener. I began learning a new skill and after two summer seasons working in the Millinery Department, I chose to strike out on my own and open my own millinery business. Private clients and horse-racing fans were my primary customers.

The Del Mar Thoroughbred Club is very popular in San Diego County. Opening Day is the largest fashion show of the year. Racegoers come not only to watch the horses but to see what everyone else will be wearing. They dress to impress and that includes wearing an absolutely fabulous hat. The Director of Promotions at Del Mar Thoroughbred Club, Julie Sarno, founded the One and Only Truly Fabulous Hats Contest for Opening Day, complete with marvelous prizes. In the second year, they asked if I would represent them by making TV appearances. They would arrange everything with the television stations and I would appear with a table full of beautiful hats and talk about the fashion trends. Sometimes I would bring gorgeous models to show off the latest hat styles and colors, and I would mention what my customers would be wearing. In closing the interview, I would talk about the hat contest, what the categories were, and how you could enter. I did this for over ten years, resulting in over fifty television appearances. I became known as the hat expert in town and was the go-to girl for any information needed on hats and headwear. Every year, the TV anchors could be seen wearing my designer hats on Opening Day.

During my career, I made hats for women going to the Kentucky Derby, Preakness Stakes, Belmont Stakes, Breeders' Cup, Dubai World Cup, and the Royal Ascot in England. My favorite interview was on CBS Channel 8, when Prince Andrew came from London for a polo match in Santa Barbara. Channel 8 wanted to interview me and my client who would be attending the event. I brought the hat that I would be making for her and went over all the intricate details for them. Another standout moment in my career was when the stylist for the Fox sitcom *Fashion House* came to my studio and asked me to make a custom hat for well-known actress Morgan Fairchild. This was such a thrill and my hat design was seen on several episodes before and after the airing. There was even a picture of her in the *National Enquirer* wearing this stunning red chapeau atop her blonde locks. I've had the good fortune to have been on the cover of several different magazines and each time it is so exhilarating. My hats were on the cover of *Music, Arts, & Fashion Magazine; Décor & Style;* and *Studio Photography & Design.* The most recent cover was *FINE Homes & Living Magazine*—definitely the biggest surprise of my life! *FINE Homes & Living Magazine* had photographed a shoot with my hats and didn't mention how they would use them in the magazine. Every month they emailed me their new publication. I opened it one month and to my complete surprise my hat was on the cover! It was breathtaking and I felt so privileged.

The highlight of my fashion career was being asked by Dame Zandra Rhodes to put my hats in her fashion shows at the Westgate Hotel in downtown San Diego. I adore her and jumped at the chance to have my hats alongside the couture collections of this international icon. It was a ginormous honor!

I joined the Fashion Group International in San Diego. It was an exciting way to meet other professionals in the fashion field. As the Regional Director, I traveled to New York and Australia, meeting people from around the world. Here in San Diego we had stylish events around town and many of the members became my customers.

My good fortune led me to realize it was important to give back to the community. I think part of running a business is to always give back. I joined the Look Good Feel Better program sponsored by the American Cancer Society. I showed patients going through chemo how to wear hats and tie scarfs so they would feel confident when they left the house. It was always a very intimate group, usually around ten patients and exclusive— no one else was allowed to attend. The patients would receive a box filled with makeup from different cosmetics companies and a cosmetologist would show them how to apply makeup to cover any flaws that might have been created by the chemotherapy. Another person showed them all the details about wearing a wig. Many of them came in crying and left smiling. It was very rewarding and I was honored to be of service for twenty years. One year Look Good Feel Better awarded me the Best State and Best National Volunteer of the Year award, sending me and my husband (yes, I remarried!) to Boca Raton, Florida, for the ceremony. I am still so humbled at such a humongous honor.

My husband and I launched the Easter Parade and Hat Contest in the Gaslamp Quarter in downtown San Diego. There were very few family events in the Gaslamp district. The event raised proceeds for children with cancer at the UCSD Hematology Oncology Department. Each year Cindy Martin from UCSD Medical Center Research would bring children downtown from UCSD who felt well enough from their chemo treatments to come to this fun children's event. I loved working with the doctors and every year they would give us a tour of the facility and tell all about the new cures and breakthroughs they were working on. The event set up stations with hats, tables with trims, and volunteers that would help the children and adults create a hat right there on the spot. I had celebrity judges who would award prizes for the best hats. There were vendors, music, and fun things for kids to do culminating with a huge egg hunt in Petco Park. We put a fence around the egg hunt and divided the kids into three age groups and only let the children in and *not* the parents. We found it best to keep the parents behind the fence to let the children enjoy the experience! This was a hugely popular event down in the Gaslamp growing bigger and bigger every year. After thirteen thrilling years, my husband and I had to leave it behind, as it had become a full-time job.

In the early '90s my husband and I moved down to the Gaslamp into a live/work loft. This was a time when no one in San Diego had been doing this. For three months prior, we would drive around downtown at all different times of the day and think, "Would I feel comfortable walking around this area?" I visited New York so many times and saw how people in the fashion industry had businesses in lofts, so we decided to be trail-blazers and give it a try. I had my hat shop there for twenty-six years, hosting events, giving tours, and being interviewed by the media. It was like being in a small town where everyone knew each other. We worked with all the businesses organizing events to bring more people there. My husband was on the Gaslamp Quarter Board of Directors representing my business and we just loved living and working downtown. We were true pioneers for this way of life.

When I wasn't getting enough business, I approached John Gregory, the Editor of the *San Diego Downtown News*, and asked if I could start a fashion column to inform readers about all the fashion events. After all, there were 30,000 people living downtown, likely most of them readers of the *Downtown News*, and I wanted to get them more excited about going to fashion shows and shopping downtown in the fabulous boutiques. Little did I know that this would bloom into something much bigger than I ever imagined. Each year there were more and more fashion events happening in San Diego. The first was when the Super Bowl came to town and a huge fashion show with celebrities was organized at the Convention Center. When I arrived at the event, they gave me a list of celebrities and said I could interview three... which ones would I choose? I chose the beautiful actress Jane Seymour and she was just a pleasure to interview. My second choice was football star Marcus Allen. I kept waiting for him to come for the interview, and at the last minute they said he had been inducted into the Football Hall of Fame!! Ugh! I was so disappointed but pleased for him that he was awarded for his success. The last person I selected was Vivica A. Fox. I stood by waiting and waiting for her and she appeared at the very last second. I walked over to interview her and reporters from two huge TV shows, *Extra* and *Access Hollywood,* swept down and took priority over me. That's when I learned there was a pecking order in the media.

By this time, I had been photographing and writing about fashion and fashion shows for over eighteen years. I just love attending these events and meeting new people. I always dress fashionably and wear a cool hat, which gives me the opportunity to meet people, from celebrities to philanthropists. Many took notice of my fashion sense and many became my customers. It introduced me to people whom I never would have met.

One of my favorite celebrities to interview was burlesque dancer Dita Von Teese. She always dresses like 1960s red carpet glamour and I adore her style. I had the opportunity to interview one of the big names in fashion, Issey Miyake, when he came to town to receive the Kyoto Prize. Only three people were selected to interview the stylist and fashion designer Rachel Zoe and I was lucky to be one of them. She was at the height of her Bravo reality television series *The Rachel Zoe Project*. It was a dream come true to meet and write about her. Grace Slick of Jefferson Airplane happens to be one of my favorite musicians. Her music spanned four decades with songs like "White Rabbit." When she came to show her art in Alexander Salazar's Fine Art Gallery, I jumped at the chance for an interview and asked how she chose her fashions during her singing career. I asked Chuck Negron from Three Dog Night during an interview who his stylist was and how he came up with his look for the stage. I even got to interview Prince Lorenzo de 'Medici who brought his amazing artwork here to show at the Del Mar Country Club.

I found that I enjoyed teaching millinery classes as much as I did music. Using this talent for teaching I expanded to other fashion classes in the early '90s at Mesa College. Eventually Adult Education contacted me about teaching millinery at West City College. Mesa College had younger students while West City College students were older adults who were taking the classes for enrichment. It was great to have such diversity with my students. In 1999, I produced my first video on straw hat making. Recently Groovy Like A Movie produced four more hat videos for me that are being sold in Australia and in the United States by Judith M millinery supplies. In the near future I plan to launch my hat book, *A Rendezvous with HATS*. This will be an instructional book on hat-making and can be used as a textbook, in the millinery business, for fashionistas, home sewers, or for people involved in costuming. There are many different groups springing up that want hats for things such as cosplay, Comic-Con, historical reenactment, Burning Man, or the ever-so-popular steampunk.

Recently a claim to fame was seeing my hats in the fashion film *Habana 3AM* by Antonio Contreras. The following year, I was nominated for Best Accessories in his fashion film *The Falling*

Leaves. Fans of hats and headwear can find my designs today in Masaki Matsuka, an upscale boutique in Newport Beach, California, that boasts a Japanese clothing line famous for their pleats. My designs are featured in the POP PR showroom in London and have been spotted on the heads of Cage the Elephant, Todrick Hall, Hayley Kiyoko, Ayda Field Williams, Olivia Cox, Cassyette, and singer-songwriter Girli.

What a twist of fate! Do you see a common thread here? Most of these people are in the music business. I seem to have come full circle and am still being touched by music, only this time by musicians wearing my hats. When I look back on my career in millinery, I realize that I've substituted one art for another...music for millinery. This pivotal change in my life showed me my true nature. I am a creative who loves working in the arts. It fuels my purpose and fills my soul with gratitude to create beautiful things no matter what the modality.

"A work of art that happens to be worn on your head" is the best way to describe the creations of milliner Diana Cavagnaro, whose atelier/fashion studio is located in the rustic countryside of Alpine, California.

A national celebrity whose credits include numerous appearances on television, Diana has graced the pages of newspapers and magazines discussing the art of millinery, fashion, and hat making. Diana's creations have adorned the heads of many international movie stars, celebrities, and socialites, and her designs are custom-made for her customers to attend well-known horse-racing events such as the Kentucky Derby, the Royal Ascot, and the Dubai World Cup. In addition to her thirty years in the hat business, Diana also teaches at San Diego Mesa College and San Diego Adult Education and offers private hat design lessons, as well as producing a series of instructional videos on hat making. Diana learned her craft when she served as assistant milliner at the Old Globe theater then struck out on her own, specializing in women's custom hats.

Diana has been awarded the ABC Channel 10 Leadership Award, the national Sunrise Award by the American Cancer Society, the Fashion Industry Style Award by the Fashion Group International, and the Armond Award for Lifetime Achievement by the Gaslamp Quarter Association. When not winning awards for her cutting-edge designs, Diana's favorite pastime is teaching agility and training tricks to her therapy dog, Lambchop.

In addition to Diana's professional work as a designer, she has been a journalist for the past eighteen years. She has written "Fashion Files," a column for the *San Diego Downtown News* and *La Jolla Today,* as well as numerous articles for *Threads Magazine*, the *San Diego Downtown News*, and the *La Jolla Village News*. Diana is an active member of the Fashion Group International®, the American Sewing Guild, Daughters of the American Revolution (DAR), the Costume Society of America, Textile Study Guild of San Diego, Alpine Woman's Club, and the San Diego Writers and Editors Guild. Diana's designs can be seen on social media via @dianacavagnaromillinery.

Kelly Palmer

Jumping Off the Dock

As my granddaughter and I walked toward each other at the Amtrak station, eager to embrace, I was determined to create a new beginning. People don't just change, we'd both witnessed that. I'd been seriously working on meeting myself for a while now. Letting go enough to learn and grow, preparing myself for such an occasion. Halfway to her, I noticed a smile so honest and open, it was definitely mirroring mine. It was Kiara's last year as a teenager and her first time visiting our new home.

Her mom and I have a challenging relationship and at times it affected ours. We'd all been trapped in our personal stories where it felt good and safe to blame and feel bad. The warm June day brightened our mood. Driving along the two-lane road as we neared the tiny waterfront town always made me feel happy. The speed limit was 40 mph and it seemed to transport me to Maui time as I caught glimpses of water as glassy as a swimming pool. I had only seen pictures of the Orca and humpback that made these waters their home in the spring. I felt blessed to have ended up in such a beautiful place as a result of reducing the commute to work. I looked over at her in the passenger seat; her smile told me she approved. When we arrived, I was proud to show her around the home we were renovating. This was going to be the type of family gathering it was designed for.

Getting into our bathing suits and making the short drive to the lake was the priority. "Let's jump off the dock," she said. There were a few things she didn't know about her Nana and swimming in the lake made me feel like a kid. The newness had worn off after the first year here and I regretted swimming less than my heart wanted. As we splashed, laughed, and exercised our bodies, I remembered that life could be this good! We explored the lake in a blow-up canoe while I told her about the otter, turtles, dragonfly, eagles, deer, and adorable ducks that made this place home. The tranquility always got to you out here bobbing around. The reflection of the trees and sky in the water looked like a magical dual world. She offered up something on her mind. "Nana, I love you," she said. "I'm so glad I'm here." Healing words to my heart.

Later that day was our girls' night out at the Beach House restaurant. We were seated at a table on the grassy patio closest to the ocean. As we made dinner conversation, our sun-kissed cheeks reflected our inner glow. I told her about joining a writing class four days earlier. I was excited but feeling underqualified; the project's 4,000-word chapter was due in a mere ten days.

"Nana, that's so amazing, I have a book idea too!" As I listened my imagination was piqued while she described every nuance of the characters. I was far from an expert, but the fictional world they inhabited was the mark of a good read. For a moment my mind drifted and I saw her signing her wildly successful book at its launch. Her long wavy hair, petite features, and beauty were right out of the fantastic story she described.

"I would love to read this when you're finished," I said. She beamed and I offered a challenge. "Let's meet at this exact table to celebrate your success when your book is launched, okay?" It was a deal.

She agreed to shadow the writing class as a fun project we'd share. The next day it was raining and we didn't mind at all; writing was on our mind. We watched the previous Zoom session where it was suggested we play a game with sticky notes to get our thoughts organized. One person would tell their story and another would jot down the highlights they picked up on. People, places, things, feelings. This was going to be a fun Saturday afternoon activity. My beloved husband, Doug, jumped in and set up an easel, clipped on the whiteboard, and organized our pens to maximize results. I was up first and what seemed like a good idea quickly become a gut-wrenching, embarrassing, friendly interrogation. The anthology project I was involved in had a specific theme. Two of my favorite mentors were participating as authors and I saw this as a chance to get to know them. I came in a couple weeks late due to hesitation and now felt I might be over my head as a complete novice. The clock was ticking, now only nine days to write about a pivot in my life that would be published to the world. Like jumping off the dock, my feet had left the ground and I was not going to care about the cold water or how goofy I looked.

I started telling a story covering events that occurred over the last couple of months during the COVID-19 pandemic. My plan was to tie in some things I learned, creating a nice neat story with meaning. After listening, they agreed it was kind of boring and wanted me to look anywhere in my life, not just the last few months. Doug took over at the easel and made a timeline going back to my birth. Yes, I did have one of those extra messy lives. There were probably three books' worth of tales in me, yet the assignment only wanted a tiny part. My husband witnessed me change over the last two years. I felt his excitement to see how I would put it into words.

He joked, "I could write your life story for you—I'm just missing the dates."

I replied, "I really don't want our company to have to hear all of this…honey."

"It's okay, Nana, there's a lot I don't know about you and my dad," encouraged Kiara.

Doug wrote Michael's birthday on the board, my first child born nine days after I turned seventeen. I fought the tears because I was still blaming myself for every single thing that went wrong. Divorce and disruption leading to his addiction. So much shame and regret for not being able to prevent this misery. It was a miracle that his daughter didn't use this as an excuse to join the downward spiral all around her. Instead she transformed into something powerful. I compared her to an oyster that had a little piece of sand lodged in it. Not just making the most out of the discomfort, going a step beyond and creating a masterpiece. I wanted to keep this writing project fun, so we ended the game here.

I still had to figure out how to put all this information to use. When I looked at the sticky notes and the little summary messages they inserted, all I felt was love. *Wow*, these two people really care about me. The theme of my life majored in shame and regret with some breakout moments of success.

Wait a minute, I thought…did I stumble upon some type of master self-improvement course disguised as a writing class? Hmmm, create a deadline that allows a person to study their life and decide when it took a positive course? Really. It was having a powerful effect on me. My mind was trying to answer the questions I asked of it. When I signed the contract to participate and was given the theme, my mind immediately went to work day and night searching for just the right story.

I understood my mother a little more these days. She became a Jehovah's Witness while pregnant with me and spent her life converting people into her solemn approach. I couldn't be a part of anything that was so narrow, leaving some people out and creating the opposite of connection. As a young person, I struggled with believing in "the man in the sky" scenario. Being number four of nine children I was quite a handful. I wanted to play sports, attend high school dances, and be offered college like my cousins. The only things approved of after high school were becoming a missionary or getting married. I was quite persuasive and got the support I needed to become a track star running varsity in my freshman year, be nominated for homecoming queen, and attend two proms wearing Vogue handmade dresses. I was in community college with a baby before my classmates graduated. When my second child was born with a rare 1/100,000 genetic condition that would leave her blind, I thought it was a punishment from God. The young marriage fell apart and I was on my own. I returned to my mother's religion and fell in love but had to be baptized before we could marry. Within six months, I became the only one in our small JW community on the island of Maui to ever need to be baptized twice. I was honest about spending one night with my ex-husband after we divorced and before I remarried. I was reported to the Elders who invalidated my baptism, which meant that I needed another dunk in the pool before family, friends, church members, and God to be accepted.

For some weird reason I became a tractor beam for the universe to continue giving me the same tragic experiences. I was excommunicated from the religion six years later after divorcing. I saw myself through a murky pair of glasses that used all my failures against me. The high school dropout, teenage parent, divorcee, and church reject were tangled roots in my identity. My subconscious thoughts told me that if God and my own family didn't love me anymore, why would anyone else? Although I appeared to have it together on the outside, I started collecting events of proof and believing I was unworthy. Not realizing this internalized message affected how I showed up and the reaction people had to my awkwardness reinforced my belief system. I made self-deprecating comments, trying to use humor to deflect how uncomfortable I was. My life became about creating a mask that drove me to fix everything on the outside to fit in. The junk values I developed had the same effect as junk food. The more I believed I could buy or display my way out of sadness and into the good life, the more depressed and anxious I became. The successful entrepreneur lifestyle often left no time to think or feel. Being a good parent meant taking care of their physical needs and providing support that kept them winning. Why were we becoming so disconnected? I wouldn't understand this until it was too late. My parents lacked the deeper emotional skills needed for intimacy and love and I was carrying that forward.

There was a great deal of turmoil for years and it felt like I had pain leaking out of me. I couldn't control it and didn't understand why it was happening. The conventional treatments accepted by our culture prescribed medications for "situational depression," like I had a glitch in my computer program or something wrong with the wiring in my head. Decades went by and feeling like a victim became a personality trait. In reality, I wasn't crazy or weak, I was a human with unmet needs and didn't have the boundaries that would keep me safe in any situation. I had to find a place where I could belong. This place would need people that could see and value me for my contribution, just the way I was. Most of all, a future that made sense because it provided meaning and purpose. My mother found this at church. That's probably why they say people who have a religious faith live longer. Could I challenge the thought that I was doomed without going to church? It seems that a religion doesn't even have to make sense for it to work. The definition of a placebo is: *A beneficial effect, which cannot be attributed to the properties of the placebo itself, and must therefore be due to the patient's belief in that treatment.* I believed that spirituality is evidenced in the life you live not the dogma you follow. My journey became a daily practice that allowed me to challenge my perceptions and do things differently.

"Nana? You're staring…"

"Oh…I'm sorry…I drifted there for a moment." It was Saturday night and I had a nineteen-year-old granddaughter trapped with her grandparents in a small town that shuts down at 8:30 p.m. I asked her, "What's the one thing you would not expect your Nana to have downstairs?" She would never be able to guess and for a moment I loved this quirky part of myself. I knew it would score big points that night. I told her to cover her eyes as I turned on the lights. "Okay, open!" Nana had a music studio, set up to be creative on any level you were capable of. As a girl, I wanted to be a singer. I sang into that cassette recorder I borrowed from the neighbors with conviction. Captain and Tennille were big stars back then and I looked the most like Tennille at Wailuku Elementary School. It was the first of my long string of failed singing attempts. I didn't show up for school the day I was supposed to sing "Love Will Keep Us Together." The next was my thirty-fifth birthday, where I was going to sing "Forget Me Nots" by Patrice Rushen. After preparing by taking singing lessons at a city college and scheduling a band, I canceled the day before my party. I'd been daydreaming about harmonizing with my five younger sisters in recent years but settled on a solo jazz career at my local bistro's open mic night instead. Tonight, the steps I had taken toward that goal provided a special opportunity to play and get to know each other. Of all the songs a nineteen-year-old would choose to sing, I was amused that it was from the Disney movie *Pocahontas*. As we sat next to each other in the recording booth she let loose and sang "Colors of the Wind" with the same enthusiasm I imagined her singing it as a nine-year-old. I listened to the words of the song and it was like she was telling a story about herself and how she felt about the world around her. She was fortunate at nineteen to have figured something out.

Sunday morning, Father's Day, we awoke to Kiara's special breakfast for Doug. His choice of activities that day included taking us to hit some golf balls. He made us feel like we had potential even if most of our swings never made contact. The slightest success was met with a huge high five. If only we gave each other this much encouragement to try new things in life. I learned it wasn't so much others' opinions that kept me down, but the thousands of automatic negative thoughts I wasn't noticing. Our internal dialogues are often so critical and undermine our connection to the world. Although I didn't really believe in meditation as other "important" people did, I borrowed their belief and gave it a try. I was reminded that all I had to do was sit quietly for a few minutes at a time and just notice my thoughts about myself. Then ask, *Is this thought useful? Is it behaving by telling me the truth?* Most of my thoughts cast doubt and told lies about who I truly was. Something this simple had stopped me from taking the actions that would lead to a better life.

It was a beautiful day and after breakfast we had plans to meet up with Kiara's auntie, my third and youngest child. Andrea had a Celtic goddess in her genes and even her fiancé David fit the picture as her knight in shining armor. We joke about the family curse from our northern European descent putting them at risk for hemochromatosis. The Sunday-morning farmers market was a perfect place to meet. The energy between us was as jubilant as the atmosphere local markets have had for centuries. As we walked around, I thought about grandchildren and genetic curses. The gene mutation took us back to our ancient relatives who were hunters then became gatherers. Evolution adapted their bodies to collect more iron dating back to the Vikings. Our Aleutian Eskimo, Russian, English and Welsh grandparents continued to pass down the mutation.

It was discovered in our family in 2016, when a clever naturopath literally saved my life. He picked up what every primary doctor couldn't put their finger on: a mutation of my HFE gene, only possible if by roll of the dice both parents' mutated genes lined up in the wrong slot. My father and older brothers recently died within a few years of each other before this discovery. The mysterious neurodegenerative disorders that killed them couldn't be linked as they were never tested. I wondered if it were possible that not only genetic diseases are passed down, but emotional trauma as well? My mother told me some sad stories about the mothers in our family history. I don't have a complete understanding of the idea, "It didn't start with me." Although I do know it's possible to influence an end to dysfunction in my link of the family chain.

Back at home late in the day the sun was still out, leaving enough time for a walk. I told Kiara the story about sitting at my favorite quiet place by the lake when a strange thing happened. "I might have discovered what they mean by a higher power talked about in the Alcoholics Anonymous book." I went on to describe what it was like when I noticed there was "something" noticing my thoughts, but wasn't the thought. It noticed the feeling of my body touching the warm dock, but wasn't my body. And it noticed my happy emotion, but wasn't the feeling itself.

"Nana, I know about this too." In her calm voice she told me about her experiences.

I stopped viewing myself as a disconnected object that day. I'm part of something. I decided to believe that there is a power at work that is in me and around me that I'm a part of. I've read that this higher power is unlimited, so there must be a point within me that is unlimited too. Instead of being closed down spiritually this started to open my mind to the possibility that I wasn't alone. We talked about all the great teachers. I told her that Jesus will always be my favorite. The theme of the Bible is love. In my own way I accessed its power by asking myself a simple question, *What would love do here?* I'd get an immediate answer which was always the opposite of what I was feeling about someone I was upset with. When I took action on the whisper, it always was the right thing to do. Like calling my mother and accepting her love just the way it was. When I hung up the phone, I felt good inside and gratitude that led me to say, "Thank you, Jesus." How could asking myself this question immediately give me the right answer in every situation? Because we don't know that's what we are made of. Life is about following love's lead, not the action our murky negative thinking leads us to. I wondered how my granddaughter would blend in to fit the mold society expected of her. She was a straight-A student in high school winning a scholarship for college, now determined not to follow the status quo "the man" expected of her. Of course, that made us a bit nervous because she had the intelligence to be a doctor or a scientist. What is a "good" life course? What will this young person, with more integrity than most adults, who only wants to use her gifts to heal others, create?

Back at home as we discussed what to make for dinner, the phone rang. It was Michael, her father. Instead of handing her the phone, I walked to the back of the house with it. He didn't sound well. He was struggling with trying another round of inpatient treatment. It was like he had given up hope. He had already been to the best that was available. Michael started using marijuana at age fourteen, his father used it and was readily available in the islands. He tells the story of how that led to his eventual use of other drugs. Like so many, you can take a good person and put them in a bad environment and witness the negative result. Somehow, I learned to section off the place in my heart that was forever broken because my dreams for him had died. The story his daughter was going to write had lovingly made a place for him. His character was a creature that was close to his best qualities of being like a jungle boy on Maui. His kind personality was disguised by what years of addiction had done to his body and mind. He grew up as a fish in the ocean, who on land could climb to the top of any tree to harvest fruit. He was a good person who was taught to respect his elders and lovingly called all of them "uncle." As I listened to him, I started to replace his identity with the vision of his character in her story and I felt a smile coming on.

When I heard Buddha's philosophy on suffering it resonated as the answer to having a more peaceful life. Buddha said, "To live is to suffer," and this suffering has always been a part of everyone's life. Buddha realized when he became enlightened that all we really have is compassion and love since basically life will suck sometimes. When I accept the tragic things in my life just as they are, not how I wished they were, it sets me free to start helping others.

The pivot in my life happened not in one big "aha" but in the seemingly small, everyday occurrences where I would catch myself in the moment. I look back on the days where I was proud of myself for recognizing when I made a tiny shift. It's really cool when you sense a space between that "something" inside you that is noticing all the wonderful options at your disposal. Then you pause and choose a better course than you did yesterday. Those moments build on each other by understanding you have a real chance at peace and harmony in your life with each course correction.

Monday morning and it was time to say goodbye. As we hugged, it was clear we had formed a strong circle of trust. Kiara asked, "Can I come back whenever I want?" What a beautiful thing to ask, I thought. When showing her the she-shack in the backyard that weekend, I told her it could be her special place. We wanted to look out at dusk and see a tiny glow like a firefly in the window. It would let us know our fairy was visiting her little cottage to write a tale.

<hr />

An entrepreneur and business owner since 1997, Kelly Shelton Vaughn found a niche specializing in hair replacement after overcoming hair loss. Her personal mission was to give someone the confidence to walk into a room and have no one notice that half their hair wasn't natural. Her business, Advanced Hair Technologies in Santa Barbara, California, took off while she was  working in nearby Montecito as the private stylist for the super wealthy. Improvements she made to the latest techniques in hair replacement technology led her to team up with the On-Rite Company, the largest manufacturer of its type in the United States. Kelly enjoys stage work, video, and international training assignments that come with her experience as a leading expert in the hair industry. She moved to Washington in 2000 to be closer to family and purchased a farmhouse on an acre of land in Tacoma.

Here, Kelly created a wholesome environment for herself and family. Feeling self-sufficient, she followed in her uncle's footsteps in developing a real estate portfolio. Over the last sixteen years, the challenges and rewards of being a rental property owner have deepened her intuition, empathy, and boundaries through her own development and personal journey. You can reach Kelly via email at kelly@sheltonvaughn.com, where she serves as a consultant for hair replacement wearers and offers free real estate advice.

Janene Russeau

Never Say Never

I was sitting on my bed drinking a cup of coffee. It was a chilly March morning. I just felt sad, my heart ached, and I was frustrated.

I was forty-five years old and living back in my small hometown. My friends and I called it the black hole. Never in a million years did I think I would be back here. I had left at age eighteen and somehow, I was back again. I knew all along that it wasn't the right place for me.

The town is not a horrible place. It's actually quite charming, and many wonderful and successful people live there and would never live anywhere else, including my parents. I was divorced, my children were grown and at college, the real estate market had crashed, I lost my home, and just ended a six-year relationship. I was dead broke and heartbroken. My body felt like I was in shackles. I felt caged in and I didn't know how to get out. There was nothing here. There wasn't anyone I could date. My only choices were the butcher, the baker, and the candlestick maker, and even they were all taken. How did I end up here?

Even as a child, I knew that I would leave, that it wasn't enough for me, this small-town life. I knew that there were many more adventures and places to see. I was an independent child, willful and righteous in my thinking. My sense of my personal freedom was instilled in me at a very young age, and I wore it like a shield of armor. I had a wild imagination and wanted to explore people and places. In contrast to my independence, I was also shy and reclusive and kept my thoughts close to my heart. My desire to leave town and travel was of the utmost importance. I always knew that traveling was the essence of life. I wanted to be free of any and all judgments. I was adventurous but also sensitive.

I knew there was more to this world than our little town. Freedom was the most important thing to me. To be free of any limitations, to say and do what I want, without deliberately hurting anyone. To be my own person, to feel alive, and to be loved for who I am, my true self. Life is a seesaw and sometimes we end up unbalanced, so we must strive to be our true inner being. I was a big dreamer and would often hide in the trees. I would read *Pippi Longstocking, Grimm's Fairy Tales,* and any adventure stories I could find. I wasn't afraid of anything. I was tenacious. I was stubborn. I was like my mother, I learned later in life. I was a warrior.

My dreams came true when I turned twenty years old. I left our hometown and became a fashion buyer. I traveled the globe and lived in New York, Chicago, Cleveland, Florida, and many major cities. I had a fun and exciting life. I was eager to learn and conquer. I was never afraid of hard work and was determined to reach my goals. I met many wonderful people along the way and enjoyed one adventure after another.

I came back to my hometown for the summer at the age of twenty-two. I ended up dating Mike, the star football player from high school. It was a rocky romance, and we were complete opposites, but I liked a challenge and found him intriguing. I ended up marrying him just two years later. Even the marriage proposal was strange, which should have been a clue. I wasn't even dating him—we hadn't spoken for about six months. He called and asked to see me one cold January night. I remember going out on my front porch and right then and there he asked me to marry him. I said yes, and we were married within six months. Back then, I think a lot of us married at a very early age, thinking it was the right thing to do. I was in love, so I thought, and he had good values and was a leader. We were different, but I believed the old cliché that opposites attract, and we had chemistry. He was a challenge and at the time, I thought that was good.

The differences started showing up right away when Mike wanted to live in a small town in Michigan and I wanted to live in New York City. I settled for a small town about two hours from where we grew up, which meant that I would drive two hours each way to work, still trying to keep my retail dream alive. He would coach football and was relaxed, while my stress levels started increasing from the constant driving. The first years of marriage were fun, but Mike was distant and not very affectionate, making me insecure. I thought sex was love and always needed more emotional security. I was strong, but unsure how to balance my feelings, wanting it to be more romantic, and yet I felt lonely. I was giving myself emotionally but not receiving enough in return. He was selfish with his emotions, and I started feeling as if I was losing myself, along with my freedom. He was controlling in his own way. I always wanted more—more of *something*. To add to the disconnection, we were young and didn't really know each other.

Life moved forward, and Mike ended up going back to work for his family company in transportation. I was overjoyed because we got transferred to Cleveland, which allowed me to work for a big retail company and I became a manager then was quickly promoted to buyer. I had some fun girlfriends and was happy. Our marriage was fun for the most part but was lacking a true deep connection. Mike was very critical of me, seemingly teasing but putting me down. He was demeaning to me and to others. At the time, I was a mere 120 pounds and worked out all the time, but he would grab my arms and tell me I was fat. I knew he loved me, but he was harsh in his words. My sense of self started to slowly diminish. I was super sensitive and the criticism started taking a toll on me. I allowed myself to become controlled by him and his words. I lost my confidence and started believing what he was saying to me. I began doubting myself and my decisions, which caused me to lose my sense of personal freedom.

We got transferred again and moved to northern Michigan. Again, it was a small college town and I found a place to work, this time a small boutique. I started managing another store and subsequently became the buyer. It was fun and I felt I was on my way again. I would take the train to Chicago and buy at the apparel market, which meant that I got to enjoy the time traveling.

When I got pregnant, I thought, "Why not?" I was happy, and I had always loved children. Then we were transferred to Chicago, a city I loved and always wanted to work in, but I ended up only working part-time. Then, I had three beautiful children all in a row. Boom! That was how I did things, everything at once! Three babies in just three and a half years. I thought if I was going to stay home, I might as well do it all at once. I enjoyed the years being home with my children, and I put all my energies into them. I loved them dearly, but at the same time, I still wanted more from my husband. He came home after work and was an amazing father when the kids were little. I'd take summer trips alone with the children while he was busy with work. We transferred often, and I enjoyed moving to major cities, even though I was always alone with the children. This went on for about fourteen years—moving, raising children, and changing jobs. I was happy and made the best out of any situation. I loved my children and we'd go on adventures and have the best of times with their active little imaginations.

We were finally transferred back to Michigan when the children were nine, eight, and six. My husband and I thought it would be a good idea to go back to our hometown. We figured it would be good for the children to spend time and grow up with their cousins, and I missed my sisters and parents. I was still feeling completely alone even with the children. I was struggling with confidence and was needing a change.

Before we moved my friends would tease me and say that I would be living down the street from my mother and doing real estate, following in her footsteps as a real estate agent. I said, "Never! I would never do that!" You see, I was a fashion buyer and an artist. I thought all these realtors with the strange clothing were peculiar. It just wasn't me. Little did I know, within a year I would be living down the street from my mother and had acquired my real estate license.

I remember feeling trapped and uneasy, but what I didn't know was that it would be a passage to my freedom. My mother had insight like no other person I'd met—she just *knew* things. She was always ten steps ahead of everyone. My younger sister wanted to take the real estate class and my mother paid for it. She signed us up *together* so I could help her pass the course. I passed right away but my sister failed, and I felt guilty; my sister wanted it and I didn't really care about selling real estate. The one thing I did learn is to never say never. Several months later I was selling homes. I started to feel my confidence coming back again.

My real estate business was booming and it was a fantastic outlet. I worked hard and poured all my time into my work and my children. My husband regressed. The more successful I became, the more he didn't like me. All the things he loved about me when we first met, my independence and freedom, he now couldn't stand about me. He quit his job, which put added pressure on me. He decided to start student teaching. I think he probably wanted something different too, but what I really saw was that he was going back in time...back to when we were dating in that same small town.

I was doing a good job of balancing the children and my career. My new success in real estate brought a lot of challenges, but I hit them head on and started socializing and having fun. Not only was I selling homes, I was a partner in building a subdivision as well as condos and building our own home. My husband refused to participate in any of it. Since my family was also in the real estate business, there were a lot of lunches and dinners out, plus social events. My husband wouldn't attend any of them. I found myself alone at events for several years. I was married and had three gorgeous, amazing children, yet I was alone.

One night at a dinner party I met a new friend. He actually was a friend of my brother. I ended up sitting next to him at the table with family and friends and we were loud, like a big loud French family. Everyone talking over each other and listening only to some of what everyone was saying. My husband was not there, and I was actually relieved because he always got angry and made me feel uncomfortable around my family. So here I was sitting next to my brother's friend talking, laughing, and having a great conversation through the night. Afterwards, we all went out dancing, and that's when the affair started. We were wild together. We started out slow, but then we couldn't get enough of each other. The sex was crazy and passionate, and he made me feel wanted. He'd tear off my clothes and break my necklaces, and we'd make love for hours. I adored having the attention of a man, and I felt alive again. I was still exceeding myself at my job and making a lot of money. I felt that I was getting my life back. I felt free.

I also felt guilty for my children and my husband. I was being selfish, but I couldn't stop. I didn't *want* to stop. My confidence was back and it felt good. We were very compatible and both worked in real estate. We were friends and lovers and our passion was intense. He actually *listened* to me, and for the first time in a long time, I felt appreciated. I was smitten.

Eventually I got a divorce, as my marriage had been crumbling long before I met my lover. Mike and I had grown apart. I was to blame as much as he—we had given up on each other. Besides my husband and my high school boyfriend, I didn't have much experience with men. Now I felt alive and more expressive with my sexuality.

The romance had me on pins and needles through the whole relationship. It lasted over six years, and I was in love with being in love. I loved the excitement a fresh affair brought to the table. The thrill of it comes quickly, like waves hitting the rocks of the ocean. It was a storm and I was living in it. The happy times were beautiful; we would sit up and talk into the wee hours of the night. I love a great conversationalist, and I finally had that with him. We went on trips and adventures and traveled to Europe. We drove around and sold real estate together at first, then enjoyed going out. We both lived off the lake so we would go out boating all day long. We would make love everywhere, on the boat, off the boat, everywhere and anywhere all day and all night.

But as beautiful as the good times were, the bad times were horrid. He had gone to jail for drinking. He was only twenty-six years old (I had thought he was at least my brother's age, but I really didn't have a clue). He was mentally mature in so many ways, but careless and immature in others, which I slowly discovered. For three out of the six years we were together, he didn't drink, making those years the most memorable. And when he was drunk, he was reckless. He would put us in dangerous situations - driving too fast, being obnoxious in crowds, always giving me a stomach ache with worry that we were going to get in trouble. I started wanting just to stay home and drink so things would just be calm. I didn't know what he would do at any given moment when he was drinking. This made me feel very insecure within our relationship. Even through the bad times, I still didn't want to stop. I began to find myself crying *with* him and crying *without* him. The age difference bothered other people, more than it bothered us. As time went on, the age difference became more apparent, especially when he was drinking.

I kept my children separate from my relationship, for the most part. I didn't bring them around him and he didn't really want me to. The differences started getting more evident, more real. I was an oxymoron: I loved it, but I hated it. I was rebelling in some way and I wasn't sure why.

Although we would never have admitted it, we ended up getting competitive in real estate. The sixteen-year age difference started hanging over us like a noose. All the things he used to love about me he started hating. My self-esteem took a nose dive and the feeling of being controlled resurfaced. I still held on too long. I had not been alone since I was in my twenties, even though in reality I really was all alone. I had always had a man in my life. I wasn't afraid, I just didn't know how to act. I was the queen of enabling my partners, taking a back seat in every way, while I lost my personal freedom. I was heartbroken, and even though I knew better, I still couldn't get over it. At the time I felt completely stupid and couldn't forgive myself. Being raised Catholic, I thought I would meet the man of my dreams and it would be forever. I was drifting through my days in a fog.

Then the market crashed. My business was suffering, and I felt guilty and awful and weak. I just wanted to crawl into a hole. And to make matters worse, my hometown was not a place you could hide. I would drive down Main Street and run into my ex-husband, my ex-boyfriend, my mother, my father, and my ex-in-laws in one fell swoop.

I was embarrassed. I was failing at real estate. Everything that came easy to me was now really, really hard. How could this have happened? I was always a lucky star! I lost all my self-esteem. I had built my own home and an entire subdivision, and I owned a cottage, a second home, and a boat. I was crashing at every turn and I could not stop it from happening, just like a slow-motion multiple-car pileup. I had let so many people take advantage of my kindness and I knew better, but what's worse is that I didn't care.

I lost my homes, real estate was in a steady decline, I was single, dead broke (again), and stuck in my hometown. I still had the love of my children, but they had all just left for college. *Now what?* I didn't even want to drive down the street. There was NOTHING here for me. I had exhausted all options.

That chilly March morning, sitting on my bed drinking a cup of coffee, my youngest sister, Donna, called and asked if I wanted to move to Colorado. *Colorado? What?* I never thought of Colorado. I took a leap of faith. It took me just ten whole minutes to say yes. I told her I would try it for two weeks and see if I liked it. I packed just one suitcase, called my children, and made the decision. I knew in my heart I had to go for it. I knew I had to do something, because inside I was crying so much that I had actually become numb. It was time. Time to get myself back, to get my personal freedom back. I didn't know how I had gotten to this point, but I felt weak and strong at the same time. I knew I could handle anything. I knew I had to try. This time, I was older and wiser. I just needed to make a move.

I didn't know a single person, but I didn't care. I wasn't afraid. I had to get out of my situation in my hometown. My sister said that her future husband had a mother that was in the onset stages of dementia and needed someone to manage her properties in Denver, Vail, and Hawaii. It was a good opportunity.

I had a glimmer of hope, and at the time I was to stay in Denver with an eighty-year-old woman named Bevy who had dementia, no husband, no close friends, and no children nearby. I actually felt relieved and a sense of adventure for the first time in a long time. It was a strange feeling, very strange and uncomfortable. I arrived and Bevy was indeed very frail, a small silhouette with white hair and the most beautiful green eyes. But despite her tiny frame, Bevy appeared very sophisticated and smart.

My job was to help Bevy and monitor the progression of her dementia. I was also staying there to give Denver a test run and to help Bevy with her properties. The Denver market was thriving, contrary to Michigan with many homes going into foreclosure. That alone was a blessing. Bevy was very independent and had lived alone for sixty years. I wasn't quite sure of the situation, but at that point I was willing to try anything. I found myself in an odd place in my life, yet I felt free again.

I lived with Bevy for over two years, and I loved her. I even got my Certified Nursing Assistant's license to help her in a more "official" capacity. The time with Bevy was a quiet way of life. She had lived alone since she was twenty years old. Her husband was murdered long before I arrived, and she lived a quiet, simple life. She was independent, unique, and interesting. We would eat breakfast and then she would read the paper and the stock market while I would go for an hour-long walk. We would eat dinner and talk about the market and all kinds of life's adventures. She was a beautiful soul and although it was not easy at times, I think we both taught each other a little about how to quiet our souls and live in peace. I learned what I always knew but had somehow lost. My personal freedom was back. Here I was with an eighty-year-old woman, who had gone through her husband being murdered. She was free. She had her personal freedom even through a very tough life. She was alone and she was okay. I could be too.

What did I learn? Live your life, and it's good to take a leap of faith. It's okay to start over and over again. I thought I was making a mistake, but I was just living. My dad always used to tell me I was so hard on myself. He said when you stop making mistakes that means you're not living. He would say that's what you're supposed to do. Bevy passed away years ago, and I will always have fond memories of our time together.

Eventually I got my Colorado real estate license. I started at zero, having nothing again. I worked hard again and proved myself to be a successful broker. I depended on *myself* this time and have gained back my personal freedom. I know now that you could put me anywhere on the planet, and I will always have my freedom. I know now that no one can take that freedom away if I don't let them. I can fly free like a bird in the sky, run barefoot in the woods, climb trees, and be free. I have peace of mind. I'm going to make mistakes, and it's okay.

Today I have a very successful real estate business in Denver, Colorado. I feel alive and am very grateful for all my life experiences. My children live in Colorado and California. We are very close at heart and see each other frequently. I always want my children to know to live their lives however they see fit. I am not here to judge, nor do I want to be judged. I am grateful to everyone that has helped me be stronger. I want them to know that everyone's personal freedom is their own. Try not to hurt others; sometimes you will but you need to do what's right for you.

I've been in Denver for over eight years now. I found out a lot about Janene in those years. I learned that I can rely on myself. I learned that I'm okay and actually a really kind, great person. Everything is not perfect in life and sometimes we just need to take a leap of faith. There's always going to be ups and downs in life. I still love to travel and love adventure. In life, there are people who just help you get to the next steps a little faster. Forever may not be *your* forever. Never give up on yourself. Don't lower your standards or trade your beliefs. I don't regret anything as I look back—no mistakes, just adventures. Remember, never say never, because you learn to eat your words. I'm ready for my next adventure, and I'm grateful for all the people I have come across to follow this path. My personal freedom is intact.

A strong childhood imagination and a love of storytelling started at a very tender age for Janene Marie Russeau. She taught herself to read at just three years old, her family often finding her hiding amidst the trees reading her favorite book.

Throughout her life Janene's tenacity and love of adventure stayed with her and she became a successful fashion buyer in her early twenties, taking on the world with travel to major cities across the country.

Preparing herself for any situation that might occur, Janene feels that life can cause you to face many challenges, and how you respond can make all the difference. This carries over into real estate, where preparing for the unexpected sets a good realtor apart from the rest. She strives daily to improve and educate herself so she can offer superior service to her customers and is dedicated to making them top priority. While Janene has lived in many vibrant locations including Michigan, Chicago, New York, New Jersey, Cleveland, West Palm Beach, and now Denver, she believes Colorado is a fantastic place to live. Having relocated many times herself, she is able to offer her expertise to her clients when helping them relocate as well.

Janene took to the real estate industry in 1998, receiving numerous awards and recognition including Rookie of the Year, Luxury Home Specialist, Relocation Expert, and the coveted First-Time Buyer Award for excellence with first-time homeowners. Part of Janene's expertise comes from being a partner in the development and building of homes. Janene is licensed in Colorado and California and is certified in Negotiations, New Construction, and Condominiums.

Janene's career isn't the only thing that she's passionate about; her passion carries over into every aspect of her life, including her family. Janene has three beautiful grown children and loves spending time with them in the Colorado Rocky Mountains. She loves to travel, walk, meet new people, and spend time with her family, including her sisters, having dinner and sharing great stories. Janene is working on writing her memoir, a story about her life, loves, and lessons. She can be reached via jadevinepublishing.com.

Awakened

Crash!

Whatever that sound was, it shook me straight out of my bones from within a deep sleep. I was out like a light, snoring away. Sheep by the hundreds were jumping over me and I didn't even budge. I don't recall anyone mentioning anything about a storm rolling through this area tonight. When big storms pass by, you'll surely not miss them. They sound louder than trains rushing by with their heavy rail cars. But trains usually blow their horn as a cautionary measure, so loud you can hear it from miles away. You feel the ground tremble and shake before it arrives. The magnitude of the weight at high speed sends vibrating ripples under the earth's floor. That feeling that makes your feet tingle. That's the weirdest feeling ever. My feet are not tingling. I didn't hear a loud horn, so I know it's not a train coming. Hmmmm.

On the other hand, if a horn does not blow, a siren might go off. Sometimes the emergency broadcast center will set off tornado sirens before a severe thunderstorm invades the town. The sirens are helpful, especially if you're asleep or not outside to see it coming. If you are outside, what a sight to see. The darkness swallows up the bright blue sky. A midnight shadow devours everything within its path. A feeling of helplessness comes over you. You begin understanding helplessness at its finest. The calm before the storm sets the tone. Everything freezes up like the dead of winter within a trance of nothingness. The air pauses like motion never existed. Without hesitation the birds stop singing, the dogs quit barking. Everybody stares at each other like deer stuck in the headlights waiting to get plowed over. Everyone scratches their heads trying to answer a question that hasn't been asked.

Usually it's pretty boring in this neck of the woods. Not too many exciting things happen around here. Just a bunch of little towns hidden between silos surrounded by corn fields. Storms don't play a fair game here. They rush in fast with a fierce vengeance, stirring everything up and showing no mercy. Big storms become the talk of the town for weeks. They cause such an immense shift in consciousness that people don't know what else to talk about. For heaven's sake, it's about time. People are finally not talking about each other. We really need to have more storms. Jeez.

A deep crashing sound rumbles the walls. Now breaking glass, and the sound of snapping wood. That's not a train or a storm! No, not again! I knew it, I just didn't want to believe it. My mom and dad started drinking early today. They were drunk when I got home from school. I really hate when my parents drink. They are in the midst of torturing each other's love to death. Dr. Jekyll and Mr. Hyde come out in both of them. They start to play Russian Roulette with each other's emotions. "Sorry," one second, "not sorry," the next. "I love you," one minute, "I hate you," the next. Their thinking is so distorted when they drink. Their relationship is toxic for each other. I really don't know what keeps them together. They are so unhappy. Sometimes they hate to look at each other. They both have these unknown characters within them. Sometimes I wonder.

Mom is always in defense mode and very argumentative. She never lets anything go. For instance, if we watched *The Price Is Right* and Bob Barker was wearing a blue shirt, and I said, "I like Bob's blue shirt," she would interrupt my next sentence before I even began, just to start an argument about the color of his shirt. She insists on having a feeling of control. She just wants people to agree with her and say, "Yes, it is a red shirt," even if she knows the shirt is blue. She just wants to win an argument and feel like she has control over the outcome. She wants to feel right and be allowed to have an opinion.

Dad always has the upper hand on her judgment. He never lets her have any say. He is such a control freak, and very destructive when he drinks. He has to put fear into everyone for control. He is such a dictator. He destroys everything he looks at. Dad's eyes get dark black and you would swear he is the Devil. Just as mean as sin. I will never know why he has to be so destructive when he gets drunk. Why is that man so unhappy? I will never know. What I do know is I don't want to be a dad, husband, or friend that acts like that. Never will I destroy everything I own. My kids will never see me get drunk and fight with their mother. My kids will get my undivided sober attention. They will not see me put myself before them. I will live for them not for me.

Wow, I really need to get some sleep. Tomorrow morning will come quick. A blink of an eye, a breath, and I have to get up and get ready for school again. I'm going to bury my head deep into this fluffy feather pillow, secure myself so tight within these blankets that the dark carries me away for a while. I hope I get lost within a magical dream of wonder. Why can't I just not wake up and live in that place forever? Why?

Awake.

The warmth of the rising sun soothes my face. My eyes open as Mother Earth blesses me with another opportunity to carry out another wonderful day. I love waking up to the birds singing elegantly. That serene sound of peace calms my soul. I really wish I knew what the birds were singing about. The tunes they sing flow right through my heart's ears, filling me with a sense of joy and happiness. If I ever find out what those birds are singing about, I swear I will become a part of it and promise that I will never come back here. Such an amazing fulfilment of grace to wake up to. Especially after a night of chaos.

Wow, I wonder what time it is? I need to hurry up and get going. It's hard knowing what time I finally fell asleep. I slowly unwrap from my security blanket. I love it when everything is quiet in this house. I have adapted to loving the silence.

I wonder what type of destruction Dad's angry drunken stupor created last night. I silently tiptoe to the door. I pause and wait a minute. I cannot hear a sound. The last thing I want to do is wake up anybody. I'm just going to creep on out of here. I peek around the corner into the kitchen. No, not again. What the hell is wrong with him? Yup, he destroyed everything in his path. He went on a rampage because there were too many dirty dishes. He acts so childish and when you add booze, it intensifies his immature behavior. He's going to make me clean up this mess. I can't stand cleaning up their messes after a long night of them being drunk. The broken dishes are like pieces of glitter spread all over the kitchen floor. The kitchen table is broken in half. That's what that loud noise was—I knew it. *Man, I hate this place. Who else has to live like this?* I hope I'm not the only one. I can't wait until I turn eighteen. I am getting out of here. No passing Go; no collecting $200, straight to wherever, but not here, that's for sure. I am so upset with my parents. No sleep, no dishes, no breakfast. I wish I didn't have to go to school. This is going to be a really long day. I've got to get going. My parents really don't care if I make it to school on time or not. They don't care about my grades. I don't even think they care about me. Off to school I go, late again like always.

Awake.

I finally made it to school. I came in right after the first break. Mrs. Smith had just entered the classroom. She is my favorite teacher. I don't know why, we just clicked for some reason. "Kids, kids, kids. It's time to settle down and get seated. Class is about to begin. Today we are going to be talking about our goals and dreams. Our futures are in the making of our own creation. The past has foretold tomorrow's dream already. What you put into life is what you will get out of it. We want our dreams to come true, right kids?"

"Yes, Mrs. Smith."

"Good, I hope every one of your dreams come true. First things first, kids. Think about what you love to do. Who and what do you want to be when you grow up? What kind of job do you want to have? You have to crawl before you can walk, so let's get an idea formed so we can create structure with direction, so our dreams come true, kids. We will start with you, Jedediah. What do you want to be when you grow up? What kind of job do you want to do for a living? Do you have any ideas?"

"I really don't know, Mrs. Smith, I never really thought about it. What I do know is I don't want to be an alcoholic like my parents. That's all I know right now, Mrs. Smith."

"Jedediah, I pray to God you don't turn into an alcoholic like your parents. Alcohol will disguise and disrupt your purest intentions. You cannot grasp and maintain the truth of any given moment. You have so much to live for, and I'm sorry you have to go through this. My parents were alcoholics too. I feel for you, Jedediah, I really do. My heart goes out to you. I can totally relate. I am here if you need anything. I see something very special in you, Jedediah. You have a gift."

"I do, Mrs. Smith? Really?"

"Yes."

"That is so cool. Thanks for just, well I mean, believing in me, Mrs. Smith."

"Jedediah, have you ever thought about writing? I see some characteristics within you that remind me of some great mystics of my time."

"Like who, Mrs. Smith?"

"You remind me of Edgar Cayce and Kahlil Gibran. Back in my day I read a lot of books. You have a special gift, Jedediah. Yes."

"I don't even know where to begin. Where or how would I start to write anything?"

"Well, Jedediah, it won't be easy, but we need to start off on a clean slate. Let's learn how to dive deep into our past and unlearn all the things we were taught and shown. Being raised by alcoholic parents is rough. I know. But you're tough, Jedediah. I learned and saw things that were not normal myself. I know you've witnessed things that are chaotic. Being raised in a dysfunctional environment is not easy. It affects your self-esteem and has an impact on where your life is heading, and where it ends up. Your parents' thoughts and views become their actions. And they were distorted tremendously. Jedediah, we are going to be the change in your family tree where addiction doesn't go any farther. I can feel it and see it in your heart. You can do it, Jedediah! Get a pen and paper and start writing down every thought, every feeling, and every action. Step by step, moment by moment. Don't go anywhere without that pen and paper! You, Jedediah, will make an impact on the rest of the world someday. Now start writing."

Awake.

After that particular moment I decided to turn my will over to a God of the best of my understanding. It is now or never. I cannot do this alone. Now is the time to reprogram the program and be the programmer. *Who do I want to be?* If I die tomorrow, what kind of person do I want to be remembered as? What kind of impact do I want to make on this world? Who do I want to become?

I remembered what Mrs. Smith said. Journaling became a part of me. I started to vent my past emotions that I kept so dear. I had no other choice but to rewire my thinking. My thoughts became the way I felt. The way I felt pursued my actions. My character then displayed what I hold so dear to the world.

I told myself for years that I was never going to be like my parents. I displayed traits that I never truly intended to act upon. I didn't even realize I was walking down the same path as my dysfunctional childhood. This made me sick to my stomach. I carried this burden around and acted out on hidden trauma for years. Deep-seated resentments controlled my every move. I didn't even realize how the past controlled my destiny. My subconscious was trying to heal itself, but I inherited all the irrational traits of an alcoholic, and all the reverse effects that came with it. I became a person I didn't like. I could not break from the chains that bound me to my past. I knew deep down in my heart I could do better and be a better man someday. I just didn't know when or how. Life became a struggle that I did not want to live anymore. I was doing the same things over and over, expecting different results. I was becoming as insane as my past.

After being involved with so much trauma I didn't even know how to live a life without trauma. I was a ticking time bomb. If I wasn't struggling day to day, it just didn't feel right, so I subconsciously would fuck something up. I finally decided that *enough is enough*, I don't want to live like this anymore. I told myself for so many years that I wasn't going to be the person I despised growing up, yet I was portraying the exact replica that I hated. This image was not me. I am not going to live like this. I am not going to be a part of an image I hate.

I started journaling with every breath, every move, and every step. I needed to start from the very beginning. What were all the factors that influenced me to become the person that I am today? I had to start writing about all my feelings growing up. Why and where does it come from? My brothers and I took care of each other from a very young age, so I became very independent and stubborn throughout the years. It was so hard to ask for help from anyone. My shallow-mindedness made more enemies than friends. My brothers and I ran the streets at an early age. We acted upon self-will with no structure or stability. We did whatever we wanted and had problems listening to authority figures. We were so poor growing up, and we found out that selling drugs brought us fast, easy money and all the friends we could ask for. This became an addiction in itself, with all of its side effects as well, such as jail, probation, mental health issues, physical health problems, substance abuse classes, failed relationships, and me becoming a man that I didn't even know. I didn't know how to love. I was ingesting toxins every day, slowly killing myself. That was the opposite of loving myself! How could I possibly love anyone else if I cannot even love myself?

Losing the mother of my children hurt. I used drugs and alcohol to cover up the pain, and I was always ready to jump right into relationships to fill that void. This was a disaster waiting to happen. None of my intimate relationships lasted long, always ending with hurtful words and repercussions I had to pay for dearly in the end. My heart was not in it for the right reasons. I was still trying to heal this little boy trapped in a grown man's body, but without a clue how to start.

The biggest eye opener I ever encountered was when I was in a relationship with a girl that was strongly addicted. I was staying sober the best I could. She got on drugs and I started taking care of the kids 24/7. Fearful thoughts arose daily. I was always worried about her. I was always wondering when she was going to come home. *Is she alive, or is she dead?* I knew deep in my heart that I had to take care of these kids, as their mom could not while she was drowning in her addiction. Hell, she couldn't even take care of herself. I had no other choice but to step up and make sure that the kids were going be okay. I loved those kids as my own.

But now the shoe was on the other foot. I began to experience exactly how my kids' momma felt. Every day for thirteen years I was there, but actually not there. I could not retain the moment naturally. I was high in another world. And now I felt the hopelessness and helplessness that she endured for years. I now knew what it felt like to be in love with an addict. I tried anything and everything to get her to stop doing drugs. I tried reverse psychology on her, saying, "Don't you even love your kids? You're pushing your kids away." She started slipping into the darkness within a downward spiral of Hell. It was like kicking a dead dog over and over. The dog is dead but you just keep kicking it, and you're not getting anywhere. Just keep going through the same bullshit day after day, praying it will get better. Every kick lets out any built-up animosity, so you keep kicking. But as the love slowly fades away, everything else fades too. I knew in my heart it was over. This very moment is when I quit writing about my self-improvement. I started writing about my experience of pain and pleasure. This was not writing about me anymore. This became my story of becoming someone's survival guide.

Awake.

I started sharing my experience, wisdom, and advice with anyone who would listen. By doing this, it helped me keep my sobriety. I kept sober by giving it away to help the next man. I shared my poems with everyone. I loved the feedback I received. This natural feeling of energy was the best feeling I ever felt. My poems started to give me a new feeling—one I never wanted to lose. I soon realized that my worst day sober felt way better than any of my best days high. I didn't want to trade that feeling for anything in the world. The energy I now possessed was awesome. When I wrote poems, my heart spoke through me. I felt the love and an overwhelming feeling of joy. I knew then that writing was my calling—it was where I was going and where I needed to be. I started to follow my intuition wholeheartedly. This eliminated any second guessing and I started to know myself. I learned a lot about myself through journaling. Journaling taught me about the character I hated and how to become the best version of myself.

If I never experienced the dark side of that other person, how could I be the best of that other half today? My selfishness created a giver out of me. My destructiveness created a person that is grateful for everything. My hate for the person I became turned into the love I have for myself and everyone. I am me and I am awake. My life lessons taught me to never give up. I now know I can do whatever I set my mind to. The reality I create is the reality that I live for love. We only live once so make it the best. I lived in the darkness for far too long. The moments of my life have now guided me out of the dark. I am now the awakened, living in the moment.

Awake.

Known as a Jack-of-all-trades, Jedediah Joseph Crouch has worked in the construction field for the last twenty years, five of those as a production manager. An excellent leader, Jedediah takes pride in his work and enjoys being of service through doing small odd jobs for friends and family in the local neighborhood.

Jedediah's greatest source of pride is that the projects he constructs will last a lifetime in others' eyes, and he has further developed his social skills working with the public in retail settings, becoming an empathetic listener and loving to help identify resolutions for seemingly hopeless scenarios.

Born in Toledo, Ohio, Jedediah graduated from Lebanon High School and now has two beautiful girls and two active boys, his oldest daughter with a successful career as a recreational therapist. Not only does Jedediah love his children immensely, he is very spiritual and loves spending time in nature, practicing meditation, fishing, and camping in his spare time.

Currently, Jedediah is actively writing two books. *Fire to Inspire* contains original poetry and quotes of righteousness, spirituality, and inspiration. *Reflective Balance* focuses on examining character, morals, and values. Jedediah is looking forward to independently publishing his work and continuing his writing journey. Jedediah can be reached via email at crouchjj77@gmail.com or through Facebook Messenger.

My Self, Your Awareness

This is the story of an African-American descendent, originating from the perspective of living under white supremacy.

No one can justify what African-Americans have been known to face for over 400 years. People of my color were and are often discriminated against for their pigment, hair texture, choice of words, and uniqueness. At a young age and as an adolescent I had experienced intense racial profiling like others had encountered before my time. I had never known the world could be so cruel until my first racial incident at just four years old.

Every morning my dearest grandmother, who we often referred to as Nana, drove me and a neighborhood friend by the name of Zone Yang to Rainbow Ridge Elementary School. The Yang family would often rely on my Nana to transport Zone to and from school as a reoccurring favor because her parents weren't able.

I recall one evening my Nana and I dropping Zone off at her household per usual. My Nana attempted to ask for a favor in return for taking Zone to school throughout the year. She shared that she had a doctor's appointment and asked Mr. and Mrs. Yang to pick up Zone and me the following day from school. It appeared that Mr. Yang disapproved, and I remember him stating that he didn't want an African-American in his car or house. From this moment on, I knew that racism and sexism existed. The expression on Mrs. Yang's face seemed unsupportive of her husband's decision and remark, and I recognized that she lived in fear of her husband, so she would have to honor her husband's judgment as head of the household. I'll never forget the look on Zone's face—in just a matter of seconds we went from children to a product of our ancestors.

When my mother would work late hours, my older sister and I would attend an after-school program. The tutors weren't encouraging academically or patient when homework help was needed by the African-American students attending this program, which accounted for about 30 percent of the attendees. I looked forward to recess the majority of my days spent there, as it felt like freedom of expression for each individual wanting to connect regardless of color. Kids were actually allowed to be exactly who they were, nothing more than kids. We were allowed to experience purity in its highest form by openly accepting others for who they were inside, not by the color of their skin, background, or community.

As I finished the eighth grade and was looking forward to attending Vista Del Lago High School, I learned about an African-American male by the name of Allen White, who had been shot and murdered in front of this very same high school due to gang violence. In history class, none of the inventors, leaders, or historic figures we studied were ever said to be African-American. It never occurred to me that the first car, lightbulb, microwave, traffic signals, and many more useful amenities that we still greatly rely on today were all invented by African-Americans. History books could never cover the amount of brain power, sweat, blood, sacrifice, and tears that African-Americans have suffered for generations in return for building this country. How can this be the land of the free, yet so many of us are internally and externally enslaved? It is, in fact, that we are not wearing shackles as our ancestors did unwillingly, but in our minds we have become crippled to our own destiny, power, and reality.

After two years, I transferred to Rancho Verde High School for better sports opportunities in track and field and basketball, but also because I was told it would be better for me academically. I hoped for a different curriculum, one in which the history of my ancestors would finally be told. Yet again I was let down.

Little did I know, my troubles had just begun as a young Black woman. When I graduated in 2012, on social media there were pictures, rants, and Black Lives Matter quotes and posts on every platform along with the name Trayvon Martin. He was a seventeen-year-old African-American murdered at gunpoint by a man named George Zimmerman. I immediately felt my heart fall to my stomach. I remembered back to the night I walked across the stage as my name was called, having received my diploma. I couldn't help but wonder why the neighborhood watchman would've thought this seventeen-year-old boy would be a threat to his life, to the point that the officer exchanged his life for the boy's. I often wonder if the officer had thought for a split second that this was someone's son, better yet that this was someone's life that he was taking. I don't think the police see African-Americans as anything more than a right to kill. We are a threat because of the color of our pigment, but further than that our capabilities.

This killing encouraged a massive social upheaval. There were many riots and protests challenging the murder of the young boy. When I turned on the TV, I learned that the first-degree murder charges that the officer should have been convicted for had been dismissed! This teenager had not posed a threat—what had been mistaken for a weapon was later found to be a bag of Skittles that the boy was holding in his hand when he was murdered. I couldn't help but feel helpless. My own dysfunctional family and the few friends I encountered over the years felt more special in that moment than any other. Trayvon's murder, like that of many other innocent African-Americans, ended up either forgotten or as a slogan on a T-shirt. It became an ongoing trend that we still see even today. I'm sure decades before my time, my ancestors suffered these very same moments to a higher degree.

Over the course of the summer I became increasingly interested in learning more about my background in search of who I am and my life's path. Reading about many world leaders I stumbled upon a woman by the name of Angela Davis. She is a feminist author, American political figure, and activist that fought for what this nation stands for. She ran on the Communist party ticket for Vice President in 1980 and 1984, and she was my role model as a young Black woman. Angela Davis went on to educate many willing to learn about the unrighteous system and political parties funded by the family that produced the illusion of the United States. She painted a clear picture of the unjust laws and related events that have negatively targeted and impacted the African-American community as a whole.

The next fall, I received a call regarding possible employment. I was aware that this company Fresh & Easy was known to hire the first twenty individuals in line outside of their headquarters. It was early—5 a.m. sharp on a Saturday morning—when I stood in line at the headquarters of the Fresh & Easy warehouse. I waited patiently for two hours before I was finally offered a position. My shift was from 5 a.m. to 3:30 p.m., and my attire looked like I was either going to the North Pole or a homeless person. I worked in less than 37-degree Fahrenheit conditions and every morning after clocking in, I'd suit up along with the other employees ready to start their shift. In this warehouse, the majority of employees were Hispanic (80%), followed by White (15%) and Black (5%). One morning as I walked into the Personal Protective Equipment room, I noticed all of the African-American employees dressed in their proper PPE, ten minutes ahead of schedule. It appeared they had been waiting on what we called the leads (team leaders) to arrive, in order to establish what department each of us would be working in for the remainder of the shift. Completely dressed, down to my gloves, hairnet, earmuffs, smock, and rubber boots, I waited to be chosen by one of the leads to work on the processing lines. As the leads arrived and dressed in the appropriate PPE, they began to pick who they desired to work within their department for the shift. One by one each lead picked a Hispanic or White employee before an African-American employee. We were always left as a last choice.

I never complained, nor was caught gossiping about our ill feelings toward the racist treatment given in the workplace. Here I worked among co-workers who spoke Spanish first and English as a second language. I was taunted about the color of my skin and often labeled "a nigger" by those that weren't fond of my complexion. I met this young adult by the name of Angel who was Hispanic and wasn't a racist. He showed me how to place orders as well as the employees working the current processing line. He and the majority of the elders were often polite and resourceful. Oftentimes he was teased for associating with the likes of a colored girl, and he sometimes defended my honor and treated me with respect as with any other employee.

Six months passed and I moved my way up to working in the whip department. The whip department worked closely with order management. It is where the food for the processing lines was stored and distributed to each assigned processing station.

I enjoyed working in the whip department because it was only three to four employees including myself per shift. One of them happened to be my reference source to the company and one hell of a hard worker—a Black man by the name of Devon Hall. His work ethic orchestrated complete organization and time management, although he had to walk on eggshells for fear that making a mistake could cause him to be terminated. He never complained, he just worked hard.

I worked alongside my colleagues for one year and three months before I was terminated by a lead from another department; it was obvious they weren't fond of me moving up in the company. No meeting was held, and management didn't care that I had never missed a day of work or that I had zero complaints regarding my work ethic. They simply said I was being terminated because my position was no longer available. Just a month after my termination, I found that my position was available again and that it had been given to the relative of a lead from a different department. Angel confronted this matter and voiced that my work ethic should enable me to sustain a permanent position within the company. Angel was also terminated for disagreeing. All the dedication and progress I made while employed there had been torn to shreds in a matter of one phone call. I remember I would catch the bus all the way down Alessandro and walk one mile to Cactus Street, then walk across the freeway bridge in ongoing traffic. I pushed myself daily to be on time and never to have an excuse for calling off of work. All this for nothing.

I began to have an interest in taking general education courses at Moreno Valley College. I found employment as a part-time cashier and sales associate at Sheikh Shoes. Sheikh was the furthest thing from a shoe palace, but it held its own clout from the various products the company produced. I was hired based on my outgoing personality, according to the hiring manager and owner. Toward the end of my first pay period it dawned on me that I was employed by a multicultural company. I enjoyed working with people from many backgrounds within the company. I heard about a full-time employment opportunity with Amazon, so I took on the responsibility of two jobs in order to afford my full-time coursework at both Moreno Valley Community College and Riverside Community College.

The majority of my classmates were able to manage their schooling expenses with no out-of-pocket spending. Fortunately, the government had granted free schooling for specific criteria. While I applied for many grants, I still had to cover about 75 percent of the investment in my education though my own personal income.

As an African-American female, I knew that nothing would be equal and that striving to be anything but oppressed would be a challenge to overcome. I didn't settle for moments of self-pity—I wore my battle scars with courage and always walked with my shoulders back and my head held high. I endured both happiness and pain to their fullest extent.

Just two months prior to the COVID-19 pandemic, I was presented with an opportunity at the peak of what I thought to be a troubled time in my life. This moment caused my priorities to begin to shift right before my eyes to create more stability and structure. At 6:30 a.m. I rise, draping myself in hospital scrubs that have been ironed inside and out. Not a crease nor wrinkle. If my contagious smile went unnoticed, at least my presentation would always be looked upon as professional. Grabbing my coat and my tea canister filled with lemon, black tea, and honey, I head out the door. I embrace the cool humidity settling on my skin.

Today marks my official first day of externship with Kaiser Permanente. But more importantly, a new beginning that has the potential to redirect my position in life as an African-American woman. As I drive down the 91 freeway, negative thoughts rob my current state of mind and take me away from feelings of peace. The question I have is whether I'll be treated respectfully and fairly. I put up my guard. I worry that based on my ethnic background, will I be looked upon as a necessity and as a much-needed attribute to the medical field? As I approach Lot #4, I realize that I should marinate in this moment out of happiness. I manage to feel a deep sense of gratitude, for this has become the very moment I worked so hard for. This would be the stepping stone to my career path that I rightfully own, and in return will provide a long-term source of financial stability. The chance to prove my skills, as well as my knowledge and work ethic, had finally come.

By the end of the month, I was transcending externship at the top of my class. I was rewarded by receiving my license and registration as a Certified Phlebotomy Technician (CPT1). Never in a million words could I describe the thoughts that surfaced in my mind—my patience had become a virtue of persistence and commitment that so willingly took over. I felt as if I could finally let my guard down and be proud of my own effort. People of my background can understand moments like this—moments that make you feel unapologetically Black. I passionately began seeking employment, applying to over dozens of facilities and medical companies per day. Within two months, I became employed after obtaining my registry by the public health department. This was truly a great moment of pride and victory for my ancestors, my community, and my family...but also myself.

Where I come from, there aren't many ways to grasp opportunities with the hope of being successful. Like so many others, I was brainwashed at a young age and programmed to believe that being Black had to be hard, that being a Black woman I would never amount to more without being considered to be betraying my own. I trained my mind to *be* the opportunity, and today my opportunity had finally survived the test.

I'd always been a free thinker and the type of person to create her own realities. Now, as a woman, I've transitioned into manifesting my power and divine authority. I have become fascinated with holistic teachings, learning about the importance of nature and focusing on using plants to cure disease in the human body. Having done my research (as always), I found that disease cannot function in an alkaline-based diet. This turned me on to a plant-based lifestyle and I eventually became vegan. Inspired by what I learned, I set out to develop a small business called Naturalherbalism that can be found on social media platforms such as Instagram and Twitter.

The core values and mission for Naturalherbalism are to focus solely on the importance of health and wellness both internally and externally. Here I demonstrate natural remedies with the use of fruits and herbs in many forms of liquids, such as cold and hot beverages, and other homeopathic beneficial products to treat things like inflammation, irritable bowel syndrome, headaches, and known issues that occur within the immune system.

This has become my daily routine, and my perspective for the only way towards sustaining a full and healthy mind/lifestyle. All of this to be done in return for realizing the best version of myself and raising my frequency in order to change the way that I think. I battled with depression and anxiety for fifteen years of my life. As a Black woman, I aim to use my platform to empower and uplift my people of color to a frequency of love and light, by encouraging self-awareness as a daily practice.

As a people, we shouldn't be subjected to walking around with a target on our back by the police or white supremacy. We should not be subjected to living in fear of our brothers and sisters. We have the divine right to a peaceful civilization just as much as the next person. Why should it be normal for us to only be of use when we are televised as athletes or entertainers? We should not be showcased or classified as animals. As part of the human race, we all put our pants on one leg at a time, and I think the change we are *really* looking for starts with self-reflection and by coming together in harmony. We can only do this by practicing self-awareness and teaching others how this should play a vital role in our way of living across the globe as a worldwide trend.

Greeted by the wind, I felt the sun kiss my melanin-soft skin, smooth with the scent of cocoa butter. A new beginning had begun. My eyes closed, visualizing and focusing on the flow of the current and the sound of calming waves hitting sand, as I grounded myself in meditation. Relaxing my shoulders, focusing on my breath as I inhaled and exhaled, the cool graze of sand and seashells completely covering my feet. Having shown love and gratitude in the existing moment, connecting with each chakra, I felt in complete alignment. Reflecting on myself, escaping the troubles and corruption of the world, I remained open to the journey of life. There on the beach, channeling my thoughts and manifesting my reality as I joined hands with my beloved soul mate that had recently come into my life. A serene halcyon, a true image of his ancestors, our hearts combined into one as he invited me to experience both peace and serenity. I was becoming whole.

It was the year of 2020, the month of May, seemingly to be a relived moment in time. Though the year had been stolen by COVID-19 and combative crimes of action, it was broadcast on the news worldwide—men and women, boys and girls, joining hand in hand as they marched downtown Riverside, on Mission Inn Avenue. There were protestors voicing their mandated rights against police brutality, demanding equal respect, equal justice, not just for the African-American community, but for all of humanity. Posters grazed the sky portraying powerful messages, in hopes to reach the heart of the white supremacists to convict the murderer of George Floyd. I was shockingly surprised to see people of all colors joined together, ready to take a stand and die for a cause they believed worth fighting for. Can you imagine people of all colors chanting "Black lives matter" in unity? I believe there has never been such a historical moment, where Black, White, Asian, and Hispanic people formed an unbreakable bond uniting in harmony.

This message isn't just to reach the African-American culture to reminisce in moments that we relive each day, but to encourage them that *they are heard, they are loved, and they are valued.* I wrote this chapter in hope of reaching the hearts and the minds of all existing under the title of "human race." The reason I started developing a passion for self-awareness is based on my own personal growth and experience of further inner-standing. Being able to continually trust the process, be patient, and learn about myself and the way I process information has helped me navigate the current with ease through the journey of my life. I can only hope that I've embedded in the minds of each reader a spark of inspiration among individuals of multiple cultures and backgrounds. Each of us possesses the skill for developing self-awareness—our first necessary step to changing the way we view others, as we change the way we view ourselves.

<hr />

A descendant of her ancestors, Aericka S. Hawkins portrays herself as a young Black activist for her generation and millennials alike, with her mission to spread knowledge and encourage self-awareness throughout all of humanity. Aericka has been developing her own self-awareness

skills, which became a necessity when she realized "it's not what you say, but how you say it."

Aericka believes that such skills represent accountability, an important source of perception which is a factor in self-reflection. As a Black female author, Aericka has noticed that self-awareness has become uncommon and obscured by today's frequency. She plans to help change the way we view others by changing the way that we view ourselves and demonstrating serenity. In doing so, we must become selfless beings.

Growing up in California, Aericka found that there are more than enough outlets to expand knowledge and explore, but not necessarily ones that guarantee elevating one's frequency. Aericka found that she was becoming a more rational thinker. During her growth, Aericka let go of carrying the burdens of others or taking on insecurity that previously had defined her, and she set forth to re-create herself and unlearn everything that she had been taught in order to create her new reality.

Aericka enjoys time to self-reflect and go on nature walks, while absorbing the written word through books such as *The Laws of Human Nature* by Robert Greene. Every morning, evening, and night Aericka routinely practices twenty-minute alignment meditation. As she focused on internal and external health and growth, she then became fascinated with the use of herbs and holistic living.

Aericka continues to educate herself and develop her beliefs and practices around learning, writing, and self-care, with hopes that someday she will be able to inspire others to become the best and healthiest version of themselves.

Letting Go

I could do it. I could tell the story exactly as it happened, because I texted with my mother several times a day for those twenty-one days—every day she was in the hospital. After every text, I took screenshots and sent them to my brother and sister with my analysis of the conversation. Sometimes I included context, comments gleaned from conversations with nurses, or conversations on speakerphone with attending physicians. But I can't bring myself to re-read the texts, to look at the photos. I don't want to know how they will make me feel. I am afraid I won't feel enough. I am afraid I will feel everything.

———◦•◦———

My mother, Richie, is eighty-five. She has outlived everyone she knew, including the middle of her five children—a boy—killed in a car crash at age sixteen. She no longer believes in God. She has beaten kidney cancer and lung cancer in the last twenty years. Two surgeries, thirteen years apart, and she is done with cancer. COPD and severe emphysema are the result of losing half a lung; she will use oxygen for the rest of her life. I don't know if there is ever going to be a way to discuss the subject of her own death with her. I have breast cancer—Stage IV. When I attempt to discuss the very real possibility of my own death, she changes the subject. I am my mother's keeper. I have always known I will be the One. There was a time I believed in the superiority of being the One, but my special status comes not as the baby pampered and indulged, but by being the one who has always listened to her.

She lives in a condominium among wealthy older people who have always lived in this community, a cohort to which she does not belong. She collects yachting and second-home gossip from her next-door neighbors, contributing none. She brags about me, but I don't know that yet. The floor-to-ceiling windows of her home face the water, but she keeps her blinds closed, shielded from the landscaping crew who mow and trim every Tuesday.

She watches old TV shows. Once a week, she gets her hair washed and styled. It is thin and brittle from years of dye, but she keeps it long and flips it off her shoulder with her hand as if it weighs far more than it does. She carries a ten-pound oxygen concentrator as she walks up the fourteen steps from her front door to my car. In the car, she labors for breath. "Just a minute," she wheezes when I ask, "How ya doing today, Mom?" I put the car in gear and drive while her breathing settles. She hands me the short grocery list, explaining the changes from last week and reminding me to check the dates on the bread. I will shop while she gets her hair done. I could easily do this without the list. On any given week, it varies by an English cucumber or a dozen eggs, a box of cereal. She composes the list in block letters, all caps, not by category or the order items are found in the store, but by the order she wants me to put the items in the basket. Frozen dinners are always last, but I get them right away, the frozen items being near the store entry, because I know it will take less than ten minutes to get out. At home, she checks my work against the list, which she asks for as soon as the groceries are put away. Substitutions or missing items are a concern, as evidenced by the look on her face and the briefing I will receive next week just before I drop her at the beauty shop. She saves these lists. I don't know why.

My mother looks forward to seeing her stylist, Amy, a childless thirty-something woman who wears 1970s-style eye makeup—too much highlighter under her big brown eyes. Amy waterskis and camps with her husband on summer weekends. He is trying to get a job at the shipyard. Amy wants to go back to school to become a medical assistant. Over lunch, Mom will bring me up-to-the-minute on Amy's life.

There are quarterly visits to the pulmonologist to review her status and CT scans. She seizes on these moments of sympathetic attention from the doctor, weaving anecdotes from her life into her responses as he questions her about her health. He asks each time, "What are you doing for exercise?" "I walk," she replies. "Great, where do you walk?" "In my house." It is the same every visit. He tells her to walk outside, walk around the grocery store and pick out her own food. She laughs. She has the laugh of a young carefree woman. She tells me in the car that she doesn't want to do her own shopping; it's too hard.

We are one month into the *New York Times* report that Seattle has the most serious outbreak of COVID-19 in the U.S. Officials recommend that Puget Sound residents over age sixty or those that have underlying health conditions stay at home. That's both of us. "What am I going to do?" she implores. I explain that she will need to start ordering her groceries online to be delivered. Richie is as tech-savvy as any octogenarian; she posts to Facebook and Instagram and follows the whole family. I assure her she can do this and I download a grocery delivery app on her phone, tell her I will check on her progress, and start the twenty-mile drive home.

⟨ ⬦ ⟩

Friday, April 3, 2020

12:19 a.m. *I'm dying. Fell bleeding phone won't work. Can't dial 911 Help*

12:20 a.m. *Help please help.*

6:42 a.m. *In room 405. Head wound. Will say more later. Turning cell off.*

It is 7:26 a.m. I see all these texts at once. My heart explodes. *Okay! She lives. Wait, what? You texted me to say you were dying? Why the fuck didn't you call me if you were dying?* I call her cell phone; no answer. I call the hospital and ask for room 405. My mother uses the surnames of her last two husbands singly or in combination—arbitrarily, it seems to me—so I list the possibilities and finally I hear, "One moment," and the operator connects me to the room, but there is no answer. I phone back and ask for the nurse's station for her room. The nurse assures me that although her appearance is quite concerning, bruising all over her face, there are no fractures, no concussion. A few staples and stitches and yes, she can come home later today or tomorrow. Whew! I call her cell phone again and leave the same message that I text: *They said you can come home today or tomorrow.*

Confident that she will be okay, I give a few hours before calling again. "Hello!" she shouts. "Hi, Mom, oh my God, what happened?"

"I texted you and texted you, I was bleeding and there was blood everywhere and you didn't text me back, so I called Lloyd.

He couldn't find the number for the Gig Harbor Police Department and I couldn't make 911 work, but finally I got it to work." "No, Mom, what happened? How did you get a head wound?" "Jim and Marjorie were making shrimp scampi, and they asked me if I wanted some. Marjorie assured me that they hadn't been anywhere except their cabin and they are wiping everything down as they go and so I said okay, that would be nice. And they left it by my door and I brought it in and it was still hot, so I sat down and it was really tasty, but really rich and they used pasta, which I thought was weird, but the shrimps were really big, but it was just too rich. I ate all of it. My stomach didn't hurt when I went to bed, but I started having cramps and I got up to use the bathroom and I passed out and smashed my head against the wall! When I woke up, I was in a pool of blood—there was blood *everywhere*! I dragged myself back to my bed and leaned against my bed and texted you—you didn't answer. I called Lloyd and he couldn't find the number for the police in Gig Harbor and my phone wouldn't work. I tried and tried and it wouldn't dial 911. Finally it worked and I told them I couldn't get to the door and they asked me how they could get in and I told them Carmen upstairs has my key and they went to her condo and knocked on the door and she gave them the key and they came in and took me to the hospital."

It is two days into the hospital stay, and I drive to her house to get the mail; there are bills that must be paid. In the tiny bathroom, two steps from the bed, there is a dull maroon oval on the floor. I make a mental note that it is definitely not *everywhere*; in fact, it is not much bigger around nor as thick as a compact disc. A single Birkenstock-knock-off house slipper is between the puddle of blood and the door. Checking her story of dragging herself back to her bed on hands and knees to make the 911 call, bleeding all the while, against what I see, I am surprised (and disappointed?) there is no blood anywhere else.

With my only tub of bleach wipes, I consider how many of the precious squares it will take to do the job. I find a scrub brush and a mini broom and dustpan and scrape up the dried blood easily. In just a couple of minutes the floor is clean again. I sit on the sofa with the mail spread out. She tells me who to pay and refers me to her check register for examples of how she wants each item posted. She will be home this afternoon, tomorrow at the latest, so this really wasn't necessary, but it is easy to be patient on the phone.

"They moved me to the ICU." She is terrified and also exhilarated. "They are testing me for COVID." She describes the elaborate layout, the protective suits the nurses are wearing. She sends a picture of the view from her bed.

"What?! Why are they doing that? You have been alone in your house for more than two weeks!"

"I know. I have a fever and a cough. They have to test me."

I call the nurse's station. I point out that the cough is part of COPD. "Yes, but she has a fever, so we have to test her." We wait only a day for the test result. "The test is negative, but we have to give two tests—it's policy." We are five days in.

"Your mother's heart rate is skyrocketing—170," the nurse tells me. "We have her on medication for that, but we can't move her out of the ICU while she is on this medication." She has stopped eating. She is afraid she will aspirate. The next day it is determined that she will receive a diet of thickened liquids. She stops getting out of bed to use the restroom. A catheter is placed. The next day she will have a CT scan. Her tummy hurts. Colitis probably, but they must rule out colon cancer. She refuses a colonoscopy. She doesn't want to know.

When moved out of the ICU, she has not eaten for a week. "Your mom isn't getting enough nutrition. We have her on an IV to keep her hydrated, but we need to get some calories in her. We have two options: a feeding tube or a nasogastric tube."

"What's the difference?" I ask, knowing the difference but needing her to hear the words.

"A feeding tube is surgically inserted into the stomach, whereas an NG tube is passed through the nose and down through the esophagus into the stomach."

"Why would you choose one over the other?" I continue. I know part of the answer to this question: a feeding tube is life support. And I know that once you are on life support, stopping it is not a simple process—well maybe it is simple, but it is one I don't want to be responsible for and besides, we discussed and defined life support three years earlier and Richie stated that she does not want it. "I could die in the surgery," she tells me later on the phone. I have no one with whom to share the irony.

She sends selfies—they are gruesome. She stares into the camera, expressionless. It is as though someone took a blunt object and pummeled every inch of her face except her chin. Her neck is collared in bruises and in the middle of her forehead sits a deep purple goose egg. She is unrecognizable. I think she must be looking at these pictures in disbelief, just as I am. She says she is not in pain. I try to decode her expression: "See how bad I look?" "Can you see how terrible this is?" She says, "I look terrible." I talk to her nurses daily. What she is telling me about her situation does not line up with the nurses' story. They say she is laughing and joking, "a very charming lady."

Each day, I review "the plan" with the nurse on duty. Some days, I catch the rounds doctor and get to confirm "the plan" with him in the room. There are two benchmarks: eating and walking. Once she does these two things, she can be transported to a local nursing facility for rehab. In my mind this is the best thing that can happen. Medicare entitles her to 120 days inpatient at a skilled nursing facility. We need rehab. This is the lifeboat that will buy us three months to figure out how to configure her life. My mother loved rehab. We remind her of this. She asks if the facility she was in before is the best facility. I don't know, but I tell her it is. My brother asks if the facility has any COVID patients—and can we take her out if they get any. I confirm they do not, and yes, we can.

The only thing my mom didn't like about rehab was the discharge process. Because she lives alone, the palliative care nurse offers her a list of community and medical resources for the homebound. "Am I homebound?" she says, surprised.

"Yes, technically you are, Mom, even though you have me to take you to the doctor." The nurse who delivers this information rubs Mom the wrong way by asking my mother to fill out an advance directive that includes a box to check marked "Do Not Resuscitate."

"I hate that nurse," she tells me when we are alone.

"She's only doing her job," I say. My mother will tell me several times over the next few years how she hated that nurse. She will hate her again very soon.

She no longer sits up in bed or stands. She will not allow aides to wash her hair for fear of not being able to breathe. She turns away the physical therapists who come twice a week. The rehab window is closing or maybe it is already closed. I talk with her nurse. She is still a candidate for the facility, but at this point she will be in skilled care and no visitors. My siblings and I talk. "This is going nowhere. Let's work it out when we get her home."

"It means I am going home to die," she responds, after the palliative care nurse asks Richie if she understands what we have just discussed.

"No, you don't have to be going home to die. Many people go home and get better, and then we take them off hospice.

Meanwhile, we are your one point of contact for anything you need—a nurse will come to your house once a week, more if you need it. A bath aide will come as often as you want—we can even arrange for someone to help with housework?" the nurse sings.

"Do you hear, Mom?" I chime in. "This will keep you out of a nursing facility. Lance and I will stay with you and we will have professionals who can help us with anything we don't know how to do or can't do."

"Yes, I understand," she replies.

The ambulance pulls up near the entrance to the condominiums and parks on the street. The stairs are too steep. Two men carry her across the lawn on a stretcher. They deposit her in the hospital bed that was delivered yesterday, using the sturdy sling on which she lies. They leave the sling under her and go. I pull her clothing out of one of three large plastic bags that come in with my mother. Her dentures are in a container I don't recognize. I find the other shoe. I wonder why it never occurred to me that she went to the hospital with one shoe. There is dried blood all over her T-shirt.

"Let's get your teeth in, Mom."

"No," she says.

"What can we get you?" says Lance, who is laid off due to the virus.

"Juice," she says. We are equipped with thickening agents for drinks, adult diapers, cleansing wipes, pain medication.

Over the next four days, she will orchestrate our movements. We will open and close the blinds, turn off this light, turn on that one. A sip of thickened juice first, then pills, then morphine. We behave as though we are cheerful, as though we expect that any moment she will ask for a sandwich and pop out of bed ready to resume her life. She takes in two ounces of liquid the first day; five ounces the second day, and none the third. I think there will be

a something, a goodbye, a profound and romantic acknowledg-
ment of the ache, of this moment that clutches us, unrelenting.
I sit next to her bed and gaze at her as she faces the television.
Gunsmoke is on in black-and-white. Does she follow the plot?
Is she aware of me watching—waiting for her to start? I can't
stand it; the next time she looks at me, I plunge in. "I'm sorry..."
I say. All of my sadness and regret is contained in this uttering. I
want another chance. I will spend more time with her. I will laze
around and watch TV. I will take her out of these four walls for
happy hour—to the local tavern where she will buy the T-shirt
that makes her feel like a regular when she returns wearing it. I
will hang around after work and make stuffed bell peppers and
we will have a cocktail before dinner.

"I'm sorry," she says. She turns back to the television. There
will be no more.

We sit connected, Lance on the sofa behind Laurie, his hand
on her shoulder. She holds my mother's right hand and I hold
her left. Three children connected to their mother in a chain of
here-it-is-there-is-nothing-else-that-can happen-now, and, how-
did-we-not-see-this-moment-arrive?

Lance asks, "Is she gone?"

"Yes," says Laurie.

One beat, two, and Lance is up and opening the front door.
"She's free," he chokes through tears that come too soon, before
he is able to get outside and run and run.

Her skin takes on a sallow tone, and I know the blood is
pooling instead of pumping and we have moments to dress her if
we are going to, while her limbs are still supple. I have known all
along what she will wear: a purple rayon tunic top and matching
long skirt that I bought her at the sample sale. It is her favorite
outfit because I gave it to her. My sister and I have done this part
before—ten years ago—when my father died. We know what the

weight of her body will feel like; her limp arm will not go easily into the second sleeve even though I hold her sitting up as if hugging her under the arms as my sister works. We also know we have to do this quickly while our nerves hold out—before the sobs overtake us. We will be able to sit and look and look and look, as if waiting for someone to give us our next move, as if our blood has pooled too, but we will not be able to dress her if we wait. I rationalize about the shoes. My brother and sister have no basis for knowing what to do here, so they follow my lead without question. I say no shoes. But really, I don't want to deal with pantyhose and my mother would never have worn shoes without some sort of stockings. She would never have gone barefoot either. I cover her feet with the blanket under which she has lain for a week.

Lance spends one more night. He insists he wants nothing from the house except a turn-of-the century Tibetan Buddhist Thangka, a hand-embroidered tapestry of tiny mirrors, red silk, and gold thread that was a gift to our grandmother. It is the only piece of art that has ever hung in our home. Laurie and I begin the two weeks of going through our mother's belongings. We work into the night feeling sick about what we are willing to throw away. There is no place to which we can donate during the virus.

She wanted to be fascinating. I imagine that at some point she was. Sent to a musical conservatory for preschool, Richie began playing piano at age three. She earned leading roles in high school and college plays. She played the cymbals in her school marching band and later the stand-up bass in an all-girl dance band. She was a princess in the Rose Festival and later, it will be hard to throw away all the yellowed newspapers in which she appears from the 1940s and early '50s. But it's hard to be fascinating once the babies start coming. Hard to hold the gaze of a man, even your husband, if what drew him to you was your glamour, the way you stood apart from all he had known on the farm. Her face was made for the heavy liner cat-eye look of the 1960s. It is hard for me to remember actual thoughts from childhood, but I clearly remember thinking, "My mother is beautiful." I am watching her get ready to leave the house, her black hair is stacked high on her head, her black lacquer earrings are decorated with a mysterious Chinese character in gold. Once, when I was in the hospital with pneumonia at age four, I didn't recognize her as she walked toward me in an outfit befitting her idol, Jacqueline Kennedy—she was that kind of beautiful. She sewed my sister and me outfits that matched the ones she made for herself. She sewed her own dresses, costumes she called them, to match the other women in the band. I keep the one I remember her in. It has a turquoise bodice and lace sleeves and collar. I don't think she wore it with the black earrings but my mind wants to keep it all together in a single complete picture of her. It seems important.

On the phone, my sister and I comb the strands of memory for a different jumping-off place, the place where we keep her a little longer and she dies in her sleep a few years later with no hard choices, no bruises, no chapped lips stretched tight and gaping toward a tiny moist sponge on a stick. Alone at night, I search for *the moment*, running the story frontward and backward in search of the instant that separates what is from what should have been. What exactly should have been? On the stack of giant rolls of Costco toilet paper in my garage sits a plastic-wrapped package. The outline of its contents makes clear that it too is toilet paper, but small rolls, comically small, sitting atop its economy-sized counterparts. The package has not been opened. My brother Lance ordered delivery to our mother when I stopped shopping for her. It came while she was in the hospital, while we all believed we could figure this out for her, while we weren't noticing that she had figured it out for herself.

I miss my mother. It is three months since her passing and some days I struggle with the notion that I could have done something—maybe many things—differently. But mostly, I am coming to understand that I was not in control of her life or death. She was her own person until the end. Our relationship was complicated, but even as the One, it was not up to me to decide her final path, only to honor her choice and her memory.

———◦•◦———

Lisa Waugh has loved books since early childhood. Thanks to her four older siblings, she was reading on her own when she entered kindergarten. She dreamed of being a librarian one day, playing at the role for hours. "Checking out" her family's books in her living room from the TV tray that served as her desk felt like the perfect life.

Lisa earned degrees in culinary arts and existential phenomenological psychology, the spelling of which she has to check every time. She has enjoyed multiple careers: telephone operator, paralegal, chef, and, for the last fifteen years, psychotherapist. Lisa has a thriving private practice in Gig Harbor, Washington.

Surviving breast cancer - six years and going strong! - deeply informs Lisa's work. Having dredged the depth of her own resilience, she loves helping others discover that they too are equal to the challenges of their lives. *Love over Fear* is her personal motto. Lisa's counseling techniques draw from Buddhist philosophy, mindfulness, and the self-compassion movement. She recommends that everyone on Earth read Cheri Huber's tiny book, *There Is Nothing Wrong with You*, and if she were Oprah, there would be a copy under your chair right now. Lisa's literary heroes include Elif Shafak and Larry McMurtry, writers whose love for their characters resonates with her deep care for her clients and their stories.

Lisa lives in Manchester, Washington, with her partner, Dave, and their cat, who shall remain nameless. She loves cooking and container gardening—all of her plants have a story or come from a loved one, making them precious to her. Her two grown daughters also call Washington home and her granddaughter was among the first in history to graduate from high school in an Internet ceremony due to COVID-19.

Though Lisa's mother was not ill with the virus, COVID-19 had a direct influence on her death on May 2, 2020. Lisa's exploration of this event is the subject of her chapter in this book.

Coming of Age

"**W**hat do you want to be when you grow up"? I heard that so many times in my youth. Truth is, I had no idea! I always knew I wanted to be a mom. Was that enough? I knew I would go to college. What then?

I finished one year of college. General education, of course, because I didn't know what I wanted to be. I married my high school sweetheart and started a family. Voilà! I am a mom! Why was that so hard to figure out?

I'm not going to bore you with the twenty-five jobs I have held. Just know that I never stayed in the same field. Okay, I will list a few of the jobs so you can see what I mean: Registered Dental Assistant, Hospital Admissions Clerk, Certified Ophthalmic Technician, Oncology Office Manager, Escrow Assistant, Administrative Assistant, etc. See? No common thread. With each new job I went back to the classroom and learned new skills for that profession. You see, I never figured out what I wanted to be when I grew up. My incentive was a paycheck to help support my family.

Let's fast forward to my last three careers in corporate America. I was an admin for the President and CEO of a famous Napa Valley winery. This was one of my very favorite positions. That looks important when I see it in print, but there were actually three admins, so my job was to make the boss look good. I answered the telephone, scheduled his chauffeur, wrote notes to everyone he saw in his travels, and shipped special bottles of wine to people he met.

There were many other one-time tasks, such as taking his extra set of keys to him when he locked himself out of his house. What was most enjoyable for me was knowing that everyone was happy to do business with us. It was a pleasant atmosphere. My boss was kind and professional. And, the customer was always right.

Unfortunately, several years after the company went public the outside Board of Directors insisted that the family sell their controlling shares of stock. This was a good business decision and increased the value of the stock.

You already know that I didn't finish college, so I didn't trust myself to make good business decisions. I asked a businessman who I had known for fifty years if my position was in jeopardy. He told me, "They are going to sell. You should start looking for another job." That wasn't what I wanted to hear, since my boss said he would never sell. But I trusted my friend. What to do?

My youngest daughter, Karen, bought a townhome in Southern California. I took a week off and went to help her sew curtains and move into her new home. While I was there, I went to three interviews. I landed a job and gave my two-week notice at the winery. I packed my belongings and waited for the moving van. I was confident that my friend had given me sound advice.

Does that sound a little crazy? I trusted my friend. I felt confident about my move, and I had a job. I rented an apartment online and had to use a map to direct me to my new home that was in a city I had never been to. It was an adventure! The day I arrived the jacaranda trees that lined the streets of my new neighborhood were all in full bloom with magnificent purple flowers. This must be the right decision, I thought. Look at my welcoming!

In case you were wondering, the winery sold eight months later, and the new owners laid off nearly all the employees. My friend had been right. By then I was settled and not looking back.

The man who later became my son-in-law invited me to attend his church. I was actually hoping to find a little neighborhood church. I had never heard of Pastor Rick Warren or his mega congregation known as Saddleback Church. I started attending and soon became involved in classes, a small group, and ministry. I felt really good having made this move.

My new position was with an independent escrow company that owned two offices. The real estate market was booming. I was once again taking classes in the evening to get up to speed in this new environment. I had to learn new software and new vocabulary and become a notary. A few months later the vice president came to me and asked if I would do the daily accounting for that office. Sure, why not? I really liked the people that I worked with and I wanted to be an integral part of the team.

This was a step up for me. In the escrow industry, the accounts must be balanced daily as mandated by the state's Department of Corporations. The money we were holding was not ours. These large deposits were from prospective buyers, and we were responsible to the buyers, sellers, and lenders. If I didn't balance, I didn't go home. I could do this! One of the classes I took in college was accounting.

Had I finally figured out what I want to be when I grow up? It certainly looked like it! I liked the people, I liked the work, the benefits were good, our clients and lenders were becoming my friends. If it sounded too good to be true, it was!

Three years later, the real estate market plummeted. The escrow companies were the first to feel the loss in home sales. We had a meeting with the president. She told us that she was selling the business. None of us would be affected. The new buyers were our current accountant and an escrow officer who owned another office in a city just south of us.

Of course, I made a call to the businessman I had known for over fifty years. He told me, "You shouldn't be worried. The one person who would know if this was a viable business is the man who has been doing their accounting for years. He knows the bottom line better than anyone." That was just what I wanted to hear! Safe at home plate!

I had purchased a home two years before, so my world was stable, and I knew this would be my last job before retirement. This was what I was supposed to be when I grew up!

One month later, our new bosses showed up bright and early and called a staff meeting. They told us we were all doing a great job, but the economy had forced them to make some difficult decisions. She called my friend's name, then my name. We were the last two employees hired. She said, "This is your last day. You can finish the day if you want, or you can leave now, it's up to you."

I was shocked! I was also embarrassed. It was not appropriate to terminate two people in front of the whole staff. And yes, I was also angry. I didn't deserve this. Neither did my friend. She walked to my desk with me and said, "Please don't tell me you are going to work the rest of the day."

I replied, "No. I am going to pick up my things and leave." We were both choking back tears.

It was the end of October. There was no severance pay, so I applied for unemployment and started sending out resumes. I couldn't work in this industry anymore because several other escrow companies were closing.

My new position was job hunting. I could get by for about three months. Then what? I took classes at One Stop where I learned how to write a resume that would get past the computer scan. I learned to go after what I always wanted to do. I learned to interview with the best. I learned to search where others may not be searching. I learned how to avoid revealing my age on my resume.

I should also mention that by now I was sixty-two years old. The people I was interviewing with were much younger, and they were not willing to take a chance on me. So unfair! My work ethic and experience were far superior to the many college grads that I was up against.

One day I was going to a job fair and I was really lost. I called Karen and told her where I was trying to go and that I couldn't find the address. She patiently talked me through the directions over the phone to get me safely there. Turned out I was on West Katella instead of East Katella. Can you feel my frustration?

By Thanksgiving I needed a break. No one was interviewing during the holidays, so I drove to Napa to spend a few days with my eldest daughter, Jane, and her family. When I arrived, there was a nicely wrapped gift on my bed. I joked, "We don't give Thanksgiving gifts," then I proceeded to open the package.

I heard my son-in-law whisper, "She won't know what it is." He was right. I had no idea what the "thing" was. Did you guess a GPS? Yep! I had my very own Garmin and I would never be lost again!

I started attending Career Night at my church. Once a month they invited employers to come and talk about their job openings.

One night I met a pleasant young woman and she took my resume. I didn't expect to hear from her after we talked. A week or so later she called and said she wanted me to come in for an interview.

The office was small, but nice. The conference room had pictures on the wall with Bible verses. I soon realized the boss was the woman's father. This was a family business and they were Christians. The interview went well, but I really didn't understand their business, so I didn't expect to get a call back. On my way home I was thanking God for leading me to a place where I could work with Christians. I felt a thread of encouragement.

To my surprise they hired me. The first day on the job was exactly three months from the day I lost my previous position. God was looking out for me. They promised me a salary, commission, 401K, and medical and dental insurance. Was this what I was supposed to be when I grew up?

It turned out this was an independent marketing organization. They represented insurance agents to the large carriers. My new position was Director of Financial Professional Relations. Everything was about image, just like the paintings with scriptures in the conference room.

My training consisted of learning everything about licensing agents to sell insurance in every state and contracting them with our portfolio of carriers. At the end of the first staff meeting I was completely bewildered. My new colleague asked if I was all right. I told him they used so many acronyms that by the time I figured out what they are saying I had missed the next few sentences. He was kind and offered to help me adapt to my new environment. He was my first friend on staff.

I started finding errors made by the woman who had taught me to do the contracting. I corrected the errors but began to feel uneasy. This involved commissions that were paid incorrectly. I came from a position where accounting was crucial. I knew this was not what I was supposed to be when I grew up.

Do you remember 2008? This was the year of the worst economic crisis in the United States since the Great Depression. Well, my new boss used that to make some changes. My salary was decreased by about 20 percent. My commissions were eliminated. My health insurance was deducted from my paycheck. My dental insurance was discontinued. The 401K he promised was never initiated. Yet he was doing this out of the kindness of his heart so we could all keep our jobs.

My colleague left the company when he expressed his concerns. He was basically standing up for me. The boss would tell you he was fired, but I think he left because he saw the writing on the wall. And, it sure wasn't scripture!

That was when I started looking for another job. I sent out resumes, made phone calls, and even went on a few interviews. It was the same story. As soon as they saw how old I was, they politely promised to call me, but never did.

My boss bought space in a newer, much bigger building. I had my own office for a few months, then he hired his son and we shared my office. One Monday morning I arrived to find all new office furniture and only one desk in my office. The boss's daughter informed me that she had graciously moved my belongings for me to save me the trouble.

Years passed. My boss called me into his office to tell me that he wanted me to be his assistant. He planned to hire someone to take on my responsibilities and the two of us would take the business to new heights. He didn't even ask if this was something I wanted to do. I had no choice in the matter. There was no mention of salary increase. His dream felt like my nightmare.

A week later, a young man walked in the back door and asked, "Which one of you am I supposed to work with?" I thought he was in the wrong office. You guessed it. My replacement. As I started his training that day, I asked about his background and familiarity with computers. He had been working in a fast food restaurant. He happened to be dating a friend of the boss's son. Well, that certainly made him qualified.

This young man was totally insubordinate. He told me I was making things way too complicated, so I should just give him the overview and he could take it from there. Yes, he came in late, took more than an hour for lunch, and left early. The other women in the office started commenting to me about how rude he was and that he shouldn't talk to clients the way he talked to me. The boss, his daughter, and his son didn't seem to hear or see anything.

This lasted two weeks, then I had to pull the plug. I didn't call my good friend this time. I knew what I had to do. I typed a simple letter of resignation. The relief I felt after I hit Print and signed my name was amazing.

As I lay my head on my pillow that night, I said this prayer, "Heavenly Father, you know how difficult this job has been for me. I am trusting you to help me through this time. Please give me the words to say tomorrow. I can make it through the next six months without dipping into my savings. I pray you will lead me to a part-time job doing something that really matters. You have taken care of me my whole life and I know you hear my prayer tonight. In Jesus' name I pray. Amen."

The next morning, I ate breakfast and dressed for work as usual. But this day would be different. It was my sixty-ninth birthday. I was resigning from my job of more than seven years. When I arrived at my office, I turned on my computer and opened the Daily Hope. I did this every day. But today was different.

This is what I read: "*It's Never Too Late to Start Your Life Calling.* If you're going to follow God's calling on your life, you've got to believe it's never, never too late." Pastor Rick Warren continued by recounting the story of Joshua when he sent the twelve spies into the Promised Land. They returned and reported that the land was too hard a place for God's people to settle. Because of their disbelief, God had a nation wander around in the desert for another *forty years*, and an entire generation died because they did not believe in God's promises. But Caleb and Joshua believed, and they got to live. Joshua was eighty-five years old at the time and he was asking God to give him an assignment, no matter how difficult, because he wanted to do great things for God.

Pastor Warren reminded me that *retirement* is not a word you will find in the Bible. We may stop working, but we are meant to continue serving the Lord. At this point in our lives we have more wisdom and experience and God does not want us to waste that. The best is yet to come!

That was my affirmation. It was time for me to move on. God heard my prayer, didn't He?

The morning went by quickly. At noon the boss's daughter brought in lunch and a birthday cake. We ate and laughed together and went back to work.

At 4 p.m. I entered the boss's office with my resignation letter in my hand. I closed the door and proceeded to thank him for seven years of employment. He was surprised. Maybe even shocked. He asked if it was because the new hire had given me such a hard time. Ah, he did notice! But he didn't do anything about it. He didn't have my back. Affirmed again!

The conversation turned to promises. He wanted me on his team. He would allow me to work part-time. He would let me choose my own hours. I firmly reiterated what I wrote in my letter. I would be leaving in two weeks.

It was Friday. I didn't have to see anyone from work for a couple of days. Each of my three daughters called me that night to wish me a happy birthday and ask me about my day. I said, "Guess what I did today?" Their guesses ranged from buying something new to going out to lunch. I said, "No. I quit my job!" This was probably the most spontaneous thing they had ever heard me do. I am a thinker, a planner—certainly not a risk taker! I assured them I would be fine. God will take care of me. Remember when I moved to Southern California? I had a job and an apartment. I had planned ahead. This time was a leap of faith.

Monday morning the new guy didn't show up. A few days later another new guy appeared. He had experience in this field and was very polite. He had no ties to the family. What a breath of fresh air! It was a pleasure to work with him, but I really wanted to tell him to run away, far away.

The boss continued to try to convince me to stay with all kinds of promises. I believed his promises when he hired me, but I learned not to listen to his promises. I finally called my friend and told him what I had done. He was surprised but told me I had made the right decision. Then he gave me his advice. "Use matches for lighting candles, not burning bridges." Affirmed again.

When clients asked why I was leaving, I told them, "I had another birthday." No more questions. Everyone assumed I was retiring.

The weeks passed quickly. Now what? I completed some tasks that I had put off at home. But I began to feel extremely unproductive. When I was working, I saved my little projects for the weekend. I finished one task this week and another the next weekend. This was different. I had no time constraints. I started one project, switched gears and started something else, then something else. I had several things started and nothing completed. I quickly learned I was not supposed to be retired. I needed some kind of structure.

I sent out a few resumes and made a few calls, but I wasn't looking for work as diligently as I had in the past. Was this a turning point? Or a dead end?

I was volunteering through my church leading the services for people in assisted living communities. One day the pastor who was overseeing the ministry came to our service. I had just heard he was promoted from an intern to part-time pastor. As I congratulated him, he told me that if the ministry kept growing, he would be able to hire an assistant. Without giving any thought to what I was about to say, I blurted out, "I'd like to apply for the job." He went home and sent an email to our senior pastor, who said, "Tell her to send me her resume."

I sent my resume and was quite surprised by his response. He told me I was overqualified. How could that be? No one else even answered my calls. I met with the senior pastor, then the other pastor, then the administrative assistant. I had positive conversations with each of them. I could see they were building a team for this regional campus and they wanted to be sure that everyone was in agreement before making the decision to hire me. This is something I have come to respect.

But that was not all! I had to submit my resume to the main church and wait for a response. Then I interviewed with the Human Resources Director. Then I took the clerical tests. Then I had the theology interview. That was the one I was worried about. Did I know enough? Was I prepared? Once again, life experiences, reading the Bible, and all the classes I took prepared me for an interview that went very well.

The senior pastor told me I was hired in record time, although it seemed like a long time to me. I really felt good about this position and the people I would work with. I started my new part-time position at the church six months and six days after my prayer to find a part-time job that matters.

Today, my main responsibility is preparing CDs for music and DVD messages with notes for our fifty-four weekly services in assisted living communities. I still serve at the community where I volunteered before I was hired. I look at that as my training ground for this position as I now train the volunteers who serve.

I love the people on staff. Our campus has grown. We've hired two more pastors and another team associate. Each was hired with the others in mind, so we make the perfect team.

I have been able to bring many of the skills I have learned at all the other jobs and put them to good use here. I completed a thirty-week counseling class which taught me to listen better. I don't need to solve problems. We have pastors and programs for that. I simply need to be present and listen to others. Quite often people just need someone to talk to, and I am here for them.

Each person on staff has areas of expertise, but we are all willingly help the others with every class and event, as well as the Sunday services. I finally found out what I wanted to be when I grew up. I wanted to be me. Working on a team. Helping others.

My lesson in all of this is that I needed to trust God. He has always taken care of me and I need to remember He knows what is best and He will continue to take care of me.

A month after I was hired, I was at a potluck with some neighbors. A lady walking her dog saw the party. She took her dog home and came back to join us. There was an empty chair at our table, so she sat down. She told us she was crashing our party and we all laughed. The more the merrier, right?

When she asked if we were all retired, my friend spoke up. She pointed to me and said, "She used to have the job from Hell. Now she has the job from Heaven." Amen.

Joan McConville has had a passion for books since she learned to read. Growing up in a small town without a library, the monthly visit from the bookmobile was a real treat. You don't know what a book-mobile is? It's a school bus converted to a library by removing all the seats and  installing bookshelves on both sides and across the back. Painted bright blue, it served the entire county, one town at a time.

As Joan's children were growing up, she developed a love of children's books. Her dream was to write colorful stories with an intentional message of being good, doing good, and learning life's lessons. Her only setback was that she wasn't an artist, and children's books require great illustrations.

Then along came videos. Joan headed back to college and dove into media classes. She found that she could produce her stories on video and not have to be an artist. The following year, a career change meant she had to relocate, so the dream of writing a book vanished.

Years later, Joan's career led her to a position working with a local church, which enables her to plan and produce the materials for church services for assisted living communities. She is instrumental in providing on-site services to fifty-four communities every week, serving over 700 seniors with messages of faith, hope, and love. Joan enjoys listening to the many stories about their lives, their children, and their grandchildren. Their stories are precious, and she can see how sharing their memories with others brings them tremendous joy.

The urge to write surfaced once again when talking to friends about leaving a legacy. Really? Write her life story? Why not!

So, if you enjoy reading Joan's chapter in this anthology, please let her know. She would appreciate the feedback, good or bad. After all, isn't that the way we learn? You can reach out to Joan via email at joanmcconville@att.net. Who knows, she might even invite you over for coffee and homemade cookies.

Gregg Gonzales

CHOOSE JOY!

Touched by Joy

Many small businesses, hit by various circumstances from lethargic marketing strategies to the economic impact of the coronavirus, have had to pivot in order to survive. Many have made various adjustments to the way they conduct their businesses— or have shifted their approach entirely. In the face of unexpected events causing catastrophic financial impact, they have used the creativity that spurred them forward as entrepreneurs to adapt to a business environment no one could have foreseen. Many have done these things under the stress of laying off employees, shutting down offices, or having to give up on their dream entirely. Financial hardship and possible ruin are a distinct possibility, and may still be for many small businesses that are barely holding on. But their goal is the same: to continue their dream, to do what they had been doing on their own terms before their world changed abruptly. They want to own their future as they had owned their past. What they have done—and how they are still doing it—is as varied as the businesses themselves. While my pivot story wasn't impacted by current events or outside circumstances, my life as I knew it was going to be changed forever, and I had to adjust fast. This became my reality in early 2018 and the journey continues to this day.

DISCOVERING TOUCH

When I made the decision to become a massage therapist in 2000, many people thought I was crazy. At the time, I probably could have agreed with them. I was in a very secure job. I was a manager working for Four Seasons Resorts and had a great team around me and even the good fortune of having the General Manager as my personal mentor. It was his mentoring that led me to believe that a life within the hotel industry was in my foreseeable future and I was set. There was one problem, however—I wasn't happy. I had been working in hotels, resorts, and restaurants my entire adult life and I wasn't fulfilled. I had climbed the ladder quickly and moved into higher levels of responsibility and salary, which I enjoyed; however, I was exhausted most days. I felt like I was an overgrown babysitter, combined with sitting in meeting after meeting about policy, procedures, and staffing issues. The best part of my work was interacting with people, both staff and customers. I loved conducting interviews for potential hires because I enjoyed hearing people's stories and what they were passionate about. I loved interacting and connecting with customers to discover their immediate needs and how I could do a better job in accommodating them. I was born a "people person" and I thrive interacting with other people. That was the part of my job I loved, but I felt disconnected most of the time. Having higher levels of responsibility came at a price. I was caught in the middle— serving upper management to whom I had to answer and front- line employees below me who I was responsible for. I managed to fill that gap fairly well in the early part of my career, but I soon found out as time went on that being in that middle space was not for me. A change was needed and I found it. When I started massage school, I quickly discovered the power of touch and it became my power, my intention, and my source of strength and purpose. This touch, I came to discover, was beyond powerful. It was energetic. A research-driven modality, Energetic Touch was a part of every massage session that I performed, and I found the effects to be impactful not only for my clients but for myself as well. It made me feel purposeful and useful in an effort to serve others in a meaningful way. The path of massage therapy gave me the fulfillment I had been searching for and I discovered true happiness.

REDISCOVERING TOUCH

February 2018: I am sitting at home recovering after the first of two surgeries on my wrists and facing the dilemma of finding a new direction and purpose in my life. In all honesty, I was searching for my joy again. I felt lost, discouraged, frustrated, hopeless, and scared. As a forty-seven-year-old husband and father of two daughters, those words may sound alarm bells about slipping into "mid-life crisis" mode, but I knew I had to dig deep and do some major soul searching. My search led me to a book which had been on my radar for a number of years, but I never seemed to make the time to sit down and actually read it. Truth be told, I didn't make time to read much of anything prior to my surgeries because I always used my trusty old excuse of "I don't have time to read a book," which was code for "I'm not making time for myself." Now that I could no longer use that weak reasoning, I felt pulled to my local bookstore and purchased *The Book of Joy* by His Holiness the Dalai Lama, Archbishop Desmond Tutu, and Douglas Abrams. It was the cover of the book that initially drew me to it: two well-known and beloved men facing each other with smiles on their faces for all the world to see. You can't help but feel good just looking at the cover, so I couldn't imagine how good it would feel to actually read their words. I'm happy to say, I was more than right.

The Book of Joy is documentation of a weeklong visit between these two friends at the Dalai Lama's home in Dharamshala, India, to celebrate his eightieth birthday and to spend uninterrupted time sharing their heartfelt, funny, and most moving stories about cultivating joy in our world. These two men—one an exiled spiritual leader of the Tibetan people and the other a leader of peace during the apartheid movement in South Africa—share a bond that transcends their spiritual titles. They are dear friends, first and foremost, and the richness of their friendship can be felt from reading the pages of the book. They used this rare moment in time to discuss the nature of joy and how it can be sustained in our ever-changing and sometimes tumultuous world. It is within this book that these two men agree on the Eight Pillars of Joy, four qualities of the mind and four qualities of the heart, which hold the key to long-lasting and sustainable joy. After finishing the book in record time (four days for me is a personal best), I found that these qualities spoke to me in the most simplistic way and provided a road map to reclaiming and keeping joy prevalent in my life.

I finished the book on February 12, 2018, and was riding high with newfound enthusiasm and energy but not really knowing what to do with it. Then Valentine's Day arrived.

———◇◆◇———

A school shooting at Marjory Stoneman Douglas High School in Parkland, Florida, occurred that day while I was still recovering from my wrist surgeries at my Colorado home. I spent the day glued to the television set watching the news coverage of this horrific tragedy across the country unfold in real time. Seventeen students and staff members were killed that day, along with another seventeen who were injured in one of the worst school shootings in our nation's history. As the father of two young daughters, an event like this really hits home, especially living in Colorado where Columbine, the Aurora theater shooting, Arapahoe High School, and the STEM School shooting in Highlands Ranch are still so vivid. Like so many people, my heart ached for these young kids who had been impacted. I immediately went into defensive mode: *What am I going to say to explain this to my kids? How do I protect them when they are at school? How, as a society, can we do something to stop these events from happening?* As I sat in shock and disbelief at what I was witnessing from afar, I couldn't help but be overwhelmed at the response from the students who survived and were being interviewed in the aftermath. Their resilience, strength, courage, and positivity I was seeing on live TV was incredible. *How are they able to be so heartfelt and well-spoken after going through what they just experienced? How is it they can show such love and compassion after seeing classmates murdered and injured? How are they able to smile and carry on?* I don't know many adults that would have been able to do what those kids did that day and continue to do even today to take on the advocacy of raising their voices to end school shootings in our country. They didn't ask for this responsibility, but they took it on willfully to create something positive from such a negative event. That, as I learned from lessons in the book, is the essence of joy.

The combination of finishing *The Book of Joy* and the Parkland shooting is what led me to find my purpose again. I couldn't sleep the evening of the school shooting because I had so many thoughts and emotions running around in my head that I felt compelled to do something. And my "something" was to write. At around 2 a.m., I opened up my laptop and started writing a letter to my daughters, Lila and Stella, to try and explain what had happened earlier in the day on television. But as I was writing, I kept envisioning the words of those two amazing men hovering nearby—their Eight Pillars keeping me strong and focused:

PERSPECTIVE, HUMILITY, HUMOR, ACCEPTANCE,
FORGIVENESS, GRATITUDE, COMPASSION, GENEROSITY

I was immediately touched by the pillars and felt their impact. These words seemed so relevant to what we, as a nation, had just witnessed, that I found a new reason to write: I am going to explain these qualities to my girls so that they can understand their true definition, meaning, and impact on our lives. So, for the first time since my college days, I wrote for the pure joy of writing. The words just poured out of me. It felt cathartic, like someone else was in control of my mind and my rapidly typing fingers. For five days straight I wrote, not paying much attention at the time to spelling, punctuation, or even if it made any sense. I had a message I wanted to share and nothing was going to stop me. On the afternoon of my last day of writing, I had completed a children's book that I titled *Joyful Living*. This name would soon become the name of my new mindfulness training business, and I eventually renamed the book *The Eight Stones*. I was so amazed when I typed the last two words, THE END, that I immediately ran to find my girls and sat them down to read my new book to them. As I read, I could sense they were taking in the words and making sense of it all. They stopped me to ask questions, they added their own commentary to the dialogues and even gave me suggestions of what my characters should look like. To my delight, they loved it, and I thought my work was done. For several months, *The Eight Stones* sat within my laptop without any formal edits or changes. I wrote it for Lila and Stella and that was it. No plans to publish or do anything with it. After mentioning the book to a friend of mine, she asked if I would mind sharing a copy with her and her family, which I gladly did, after pleading with her not to judge too harshly since I am a novice at writing. A day after she received the book, she called me to say how amazing it was and how much her kids absolutely loved it. She then asked if she could purchase a copy of the book once it was published and I was floored. I had to go back and read it once again, just to see if she was just being overly kind. I have to say, I was quite happy with what I read. For the first time in my life, I felt confident that I could actually write and publish a book of my own to share with the world. Beyond that, I realized that my ability to positively impact people's lives through touching them energetically, rather than physically, was a distinct possibility.

This was the moment that my pivot happened. The feeling of purposefulness and usefulness combined with doing work that was authentic and genuine to who I am became clear. The possibilities of what Joyful Living as a business could become was coming into fruition and my new journey towards giving to others had begun. Any type of work that I pursued had to be authentic to who I was and express the passion in me to help others. The book that I wrote became a newfound catalyst for teaching and sharing my knowledge of mindfulness to others as a pathway to sustaining joy. Soon after completing the first draft of my business plan, I began a new journey towards mindful journaling as not only a means of bringing presence to my life, but also to compile and capture my many thoughts, energies, and visions of what my new career path would entail. Over the years, my work has developed into various formats: workshops, retreats, one-on-one and group training programs, outdoor experiences, Joy Supper Clubs, and so on. My clients have included stay-at-home moms, executive-level managers and business owners, veterans, and senior citizens. I've extended my work into helping those suffering from addiction and recovery, domestic violence, mental health struggles, as well as at-risk children, teens, and young adults. To be able to impact such a wide array of people through my work has been an absolute joy to experience. With each interaction, I realized that the energy and intention I brought to all of my Joyful Living work was similar to the energy and intention I made part of every massage therapy session I conducted. The power of Energetic Touch and conscious connection was present in everything while I created the vision and mission of Joyful Living. But how exactly do they apply to my work and what are they specifically?

ENERGETIC TOUCH

Energetic Touch is a combination of twenty-plus years of study, research, and training in hands-on, and more specifically hands-off, healing. Energetic Touch is a holistic, evidence-based therapy that incorporates the science of quantum physics with the intentional and compassionate use of universal energy. Each treatment uses the practitioner as a conduit to a loving healing touch in order to release any pain and blocks in a person's body. Energetic Touch has been used in blending of the modalities of Healing Touch, Therapeutic Touch, Quantum Touch, Shamanic Touch, Spiritual Healing, and countless other techniques and modalities within the spectrum of bodywork, but I tend to utilize the same principles within my scope of dialogue work.

Energetic Touch approaches healing in a unique way that brings science and spirituality together to improve health in a wide variety of conditions. This healing alters our DNA and brings harmony and unity into our cells, returning them to a natural state of balance and equilibrium. Energetic Touch uses the gift of touch to influence the human energy system, specifically the energy field that surrounds the body, and the energy centers that control the flow from the energy field to the physical body. It is always based on the caring relationship in which the practitioner and client come together energetically to facilitate the client's health and healing.

Energetic Touch is consciously using hands in a non-invasive, scientific yet heart-centered and intentional way to release blocks in order to support and facilitate physical, emotional, mental, and spiritual well-being. The goal of Energetic Touch is to restore balance and harmonies in the energy system, placing the client in a position to self-heal. My connection to this modality came fairly easy and it became a signature focus of my work within the scope of massage therapy. However, I believe that positive, energetic touch is possible in any circumstance, such as an intentional handshake, a kind hand on a shoulder of someone in need, and the heartfelt embrace of a loved one.

CONSCIOUS CONNECTION

My conscious connection journey began simply through journaling. I have never been a prolific writer and staring at a blank page to capture my thoughts and feelings was an uncomfortable exercise for me. However, I found that through mindful concentration and asking myself inquisitive and heart-centered questions, the process of journaling became not only enjoyable but also very therapeutic as well. Here are the steps I took when I started my own journaling practice and I now incorporate these into my Joyful Living sessions as well:

Step 1: Make the decision to participate fully. Once you choose to start, it is important to realize you are making an investment in yourself. This process will take time, commitment, and dedication to not only completing it fully, but also to see the lasting benefits for yourself. I think of it like joining a gym to get in shape or writing a book you've always wanted to write. The end result is not necessarily the goal—it is the process of self-discovery that will bring you noticeable changes within yourself as you continue on this journey.

Step 2: Find a blank notebook or journal that is to be used specifically for this exercise. Use a book that has a special feel, a certain texture, a particular weight that makes it a unique writing tool for yourself. A spiral notebook you used back in school is not recommended. For suggestions and recommendations for notebooks, reach out and I'll tell you some of my go-to journaling tools. Now find a favorite pen and make sure you have several. Find a pen that feels good to hold and writes in a way that you like. Just as a violinist has their Stradivarius, these are your instruments and tools you will need as you create your own work of art.

Step 3: Start simply with just five questions each week. Keep the questions near you as you work through them each week to review and reflect on your answers as you journal. You can come back to them again and again once you've completed the exercises and start the process all over again. It's enlightening to see how my answers have evolved and changed after time has passed!

Step 4: With your weekly questions in hand, follow these simple instructions:
   a. Before you start, make yourself a warm beverage. Grab your favorite journal and pen.
   b. Make sure you have made time for yourself to be present and mindful. Find a quiet space, outdoors in nature or near a window if possible.

c. Pause and close your eyes. Breathe deeply three times, creating a space of openness and honesty within your heart as well as quieting and slowing down your mind.

d. When you are ready, open your eyes and read the questions carefully. Don't search for the "right" answer—search for YOUR answer, right here and now.

e. Begin to write your answers.

Step 5: After you have completed the first set of questions for the week, I recommend setting your journal aside for a few days and then go back to review your answers. Try not to feel compelled to change or rewrite your answers. Remember, these are a snapshot of your life in that moment, a period of mindfulness you created for yourself to answer fully and honestly. Reflect with openness and with a kind heart. Continue this process each week to continue to unlock the secrets to mental strength and lasting joy to lift and support you through the years ahead.

I quickly found that by doing this exercise, I was able to:

- Improve my self-esteem and develop a stronger relationship with myself and others.
- Embody my own strengths and gifts.
- Strengthen my mindfulness muscles to increase presence within myself and others.
- Learn to listen from a deeper and more self-aware space.
- Express myself more fully and authentically.
- Develop stronger listening skills, increase my focus, and become a better communicator.
- Increase my ability to find my own voice in order to speak in front of people.
- Learn to and be comfortable with telling my own story.

- Express myself openly and honestly.
- Realize my highest potential in everything I set my mind to achieving.

There is nothing that replaces human connection and nothing is going to get you farther along than being able to connect with people. There is no area of your life—whether it be work or personal interaction—that you are not going to benefit by communicating effectively and authentically. But it has to start with making the connection to yourself and your own story.

TOUCHED BY JOY

It is now my mission to continue the work of His Holiness the Dalai Lama and Archbishop Desmond Tutu by spreading the message of joy and teaching people how to find, keep, and share their joy with others through conscious connection and Energetic Touch. Through workshops, public speaking, journals, books, podcasts, and vid-casts, as well as in-person and online courses, my work within Joyful Living continues the path that these two amazing men brought to light by showing how to sustain joy in a world that so desperately needs it. From countless people I've spoken to since the beginning of Joyful Living, I know there is a growing need in our society to focus on joy and keep it prevalent, especially in times of crisis and struggle.

Over these last few months, we've all been faced with a new way of living that we couldn't have expected nor prepared for. We find ourselves thrust into this new reality of uncertainty and unease, and our connections to ourselves, our closest friends and family, our way of living, and our vision for the future are being tested every day. To keep these connections strong, it takes a conscious commitment to aligning our thoughts and actions with what we value most. To help people live their most joyful life possible during and after these challenging times, it is my daily mission to build and strengthen the important connections within people's lives—to themselves and to others. My lesson has been this: in order to positively impact another human being, the act of intentional touch is required—whether that be positive physical touch or energetically given—and its impact can change people's lives, especially yours.

———◦•◦———

Connections are some of the most important things in life. Gregg Gonzales, founder of Joyful Living LLC, has learned firsthand that the connections you make with others don't happen until you start connecting to yourself first. An internationally known mindfulness trainer, researcher, speaker, and author, Gregg's mission is to spread con-  tagious joy through mindfulness training practices that are centered on creating *connections* as the gateway to lasting joy and happiness. His unique and effective connection techniques have been utilized in both one-on-one and group training programs, workshops, and retreats, as well as charitable and nonprofit initiatives that are close to his heart.

Gregg's path began in middle school when he was invited to participate in a new peer counseling program that brought him face-to-face with fellow students who felt challenged and disconnected. He recognized then, just as he does now, that his ability to connect with others in a compassionate, open, and heart-centered space was the key to providing support and guidance to others. As a natural empath and giver, Gregg has dedicated his work to helping those who are searching for life purpose, direction, and fulfillment. Gregg's impactful teachings have been inspired by his mentors, such as Jack Kornfield, Simon Sinek, Jen Sincero, Archbishop Desmond Tutu, and His Holiness the Dalai Lama.

Gregg believes that there are four keys to consciously connecting, which he emphasizes in his work: attentive listening, respect, integrity, and loving-kindness. It is his mission to show how useful these valuable keys are in every connection we have in our daily lives—with loved ones, friends, co-workers, strangers, and especially with ourselves.

Gregg lives in Aurora, Colorado, with his wife, Barbara, and his two daughters, Lila and Stella—the inspirations for creating Joyful Living in 2018.

Acknowledgments

First and foremost, I am deeply grateful that I have been Divinely guided to help writers become authors and share my talents with others. I am truly thankful for all the amazing people in my life, including my clients, friends and family.

Thank you to my family – Mom, Dad, Jane, Andrew, Zach, Karen and Mat, for their love and support as I set sail into the next phase of my life, following a giant pivot of my own when I moved back to California. I am finally home. Special thanks to my mom, Joan (Bunny) McConville, for bringing me into this world and always giving love freely...not just to me, but to everyone in her life. You make me a better person with your daily demonstration of faith, love and compassion.

Thank you to Stacy and Farrell Rodrigues, and Peggy Graham, for being my second family and for Stacy nudging me (actually more like tough love) to create Finish the Book Publishing. Pineapple Power! There is definitely wine in our future.

Many heartfelt thanks to M. Shannon Hernandez and The Confident Expert tribe. Your wisdom, dedication and perseverance with each of your respective businesses inspire me to keep moving forward, and I learn something new from you each and every day.

Thank you to the team that helped *The Pivot Project* come to life – James Ranson, Amy Scott and Michelle White, and for their expertise and being a part of something awesome. Thank you, Gail Manahan, for and sharing your publishing experience and your perspective on becoming an author. You have a special place in my heart.

To the contributing authors of *The Pivot Project* – THANK YOU Aericka, Diana, Georgia, Gregg, Jane, Janene, Jedediah, Joan, Kelly and Lisa - each of you have been a shining light in my life, and I am blessed by your friendship. You are the reason this book has been created. I am deeply humbled that you had trust in me to share your stories with the world and I am grateful to have walked the path with you.

In honor of contributing author Lisa Waugh and all those who have endured a diagnosis of cancer, a portion of the proceeds from this book will be donated to the American Cancer Society.

We send you healing love and prayers that your health will be fully restored to continue on your own journey. Donations can be made at cancer.org.

Susie Schaefer

About the Author

Susie Schaefer's love of books goes far beyond the feel of a fabric cover or the smell of a library. Her passion for helping authors put out high quality books and market them successfully brings her tremendous joy — especially when they become an Amazon Best Seller.

Susie hails from three decades in corporate America — teaching and training, becoming a marketing expert, working with non-profits, and in radio broadcasting and commercial acting. Susie has been called a "God-send" by her clients and skillfully guides authors through the independent publishing process to finish that dream book, launch a speaking career, or build an entrepreneurial business.

Susie teaches workshops and shares her publishing expertise for a variety of writing and publishing groups nationwide, and is honored to be a judge for the Independent Book Publisher's Association's Benjamin Franklin Book Awards. When not reading, reviewing, or publishing books, Susie can be found practicing her downward dog (yoga), meditating on the beach, or planning her next travel adventure.

FINISH THE BOOK PUBLISHING SERVICES INCLUDE:

- The **Behind the Scenes** Program, which takes a group of authors through writing, editing, design, publishing and book marketing, while contributing a single chapter to create a themed anthology.
- **Author Evolution,** a monthly group membership that empowers authors in an online collaborative environment to ask those burning questions and get answers related to independent publishing.
- The **Amazon Best Seller Campaign,** a service for published authors to get their books positioned for Best Seller status and future book marketing.
- **One-on-one publishing services** to help you create your desired book and successfully publish independently, keeping 100% of your rights and royalties.

Complimentary 30-minute consultations
are available to discover your next steps to becoming
an independently published author.

To find out how to connect, visit
www.FinishTheBookPublishing.com.